ALL RIGHTS OF THE MANUFACTURER AND OF THE OWNER OF THE RECORDED WORK RESERVED. UNAUTHORISED PUBLIC PERFORMANCE, BROADCASTING AND COPYING OF THIS RECORD PROHIBITED.
OAK REGD.
DEMODISC by
R. G. JONES
OF MORDEN
LTD.,
MORDEN,
SURREY
OAK
RECORDS
45 rpm
RGJ 407
Made in England
THE ACT
TURN TO LOVE YOU.
I WARNED YOU.

Sonic Antiquarian

Thee (Un)Complete Rockhunter

by

Thee Rockhunter

Produced by The LedaTape Organisation
on behalf of the author.

November 2011

BOOK
PRODUCTION
WAR ECONOMY
STANDARD

This book has been produced
in complete conformity with the
authorised economy standards

I

Introdcution

Ultimate Ancient Historical Everlivin' Feedback Riff-Up

Yeah, you heard!!! Antiquarian rockin' sounds 'n' nuthin' else!!! I'm bringin' it back home!!! Doin' it for a time when The Past itself runs out of juice.

Lemme get you started… and keep the engine running, mush. This is all about a two-sided A4 fanzine I used to make. Some called it Rockhunter. I used to distribute this thing down the Heart & Hand pub, Brighton, with a few copies left in Borderline, just over the road.

The story is that way back no one really knew who made all the truly great, distant-sounding recordings of Rock 'n' Roll Yore. These great works circumscribed the lost possible of imagined sounds and put experience in a different order. They were myths, hyped and archived by their even more distant collectors who survived on new antiquity, fresh scarcity, aether and wish sandwiches, washed down with pure conceit.

Back then I was busy re-digging the vivid olden language of loss of garage punk compilation LP sleeve notes. Plus invisible sounds. All that stuff still makes me weep. I couldn't help picking at the stinky puke scab of actual history. By the end of my Rockhunting I'd steamrollered, bulldozed and punified the standard myths of rock 'n' roll. I was paying homage to what might never have been if it weren't for me making it.

This was natural history more than some milquetoaste journalistic leg-up. I wasn't going nowhere. I still aren't. I was guided by the invisible light. Beckoned forwards by the good stuff that isn't here yet — and all the stuff waiting to be born that people haven't quite got round to invoking. I can see it.

I liked handing issues of Rockhunter over personally, then gauging the beautiful look in the eyes of the beholder — whether it be fear, uncertainty, horror, embarrassment or, worse and most piquant and terrible of all the emotions, disappointment.

I could mention Myles Na gCopaleen, James Frazer, Angela Carter, Colin Wilson, Lester Bangs, Ezra Pound, Doreen Massey, Céline, Lee Perry, Michael Moorcock and a whole buncha others. But that would only get me halfway further to not being grokked any less better than I'm not already.

Anyway, what was I going on about? Oh yeah, who am I? Dig my howlin' works ye ones who reckon ye're pretty mighty — and ye ones who insist on making others feel mighty over and over again throughout the history of humanity — and die!!!!

Three love,
Your Editor

Note

Nos. 1-3 (June 1992, March 1994 and June 1996) were typed and printed, No. 4 was typed and photocopied (Somewhere between September 1997 and July 1999, but things had grown hazy and I can't remember the dates.) These were glossy covered 20-30 page mags with black and white pics. Except for No. 4, the "breakdown" issue, which featured a glossy cover on a dozen pages of very closely handwritten and typed text, the meanings of which are a little bit uncertain. You'll find reproductions of the original cover art for Nos. 1 to 4, blotches, botches 'n' all, nestled in the following pages.

The text for issues 1 to 4 is still only available in archived print copies. The effort-to-reward ratio necessary to extract the text from these issues was too slight, even for me.

Nos. 5-18 were done on a PC and laser-printed then photocopied as coverless newsletters. Anything from No. 19 on was issued first as internet text.

ROCKHUNTER
NUMBER 1
HP LOVECRAFT VS. THEE HEADCOATS
FEN PUNK FANTOMS
APOCALYPSE PSYKE
THE ENGLISH DIMENSION
£2.50

1

June 1992

2

March 1994

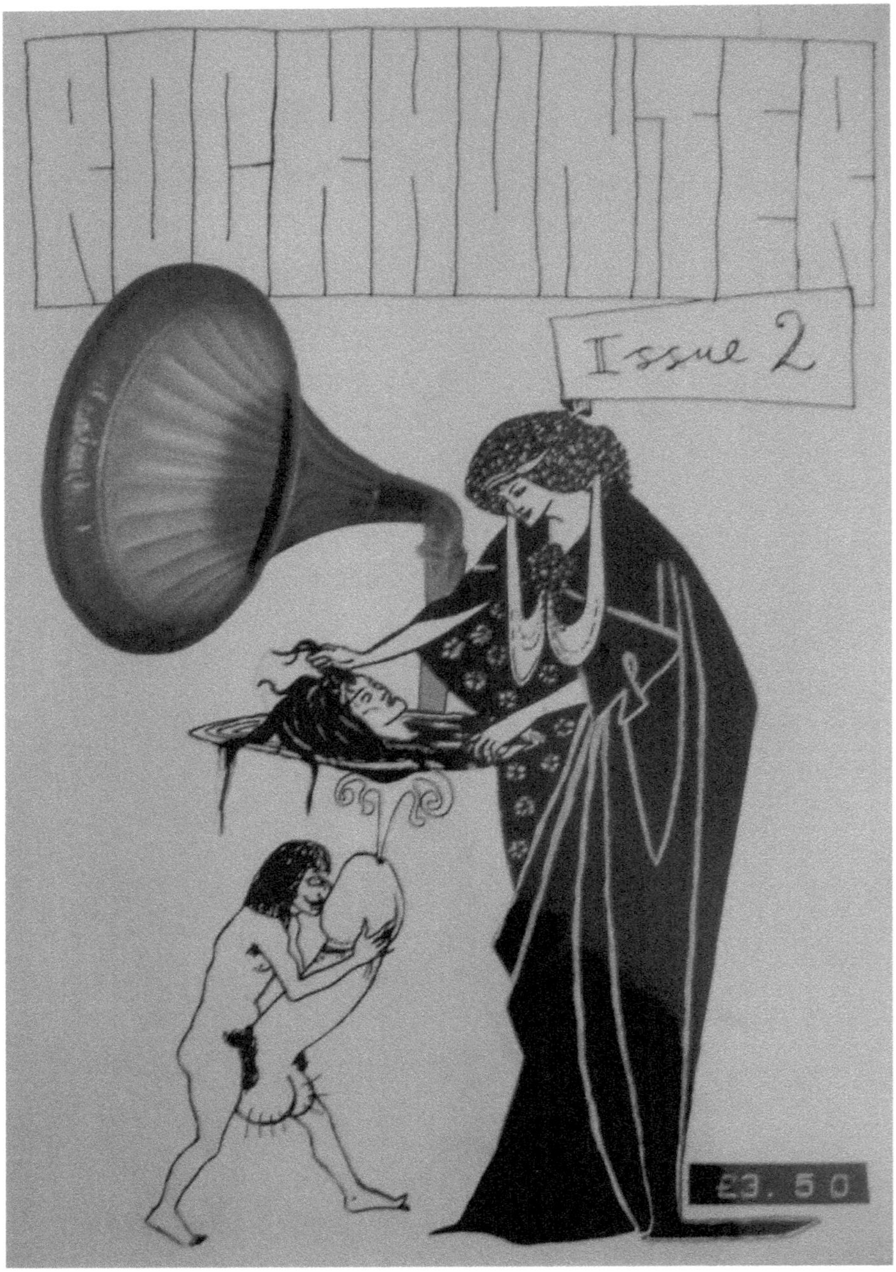

Rockhunter
ISSUE 3
HISTORY OF FEN PUNK 3
£3.50
ST JOHNS TAVERN
NEO LEGENDARY BEAT HAVEN
NO CDS
PLUS. . .LIVE SOUNDZ N RECORD REVIEWZ

3

June 1996

4

c. 1998

5

September 2003

Greasers Doin' The Boogie
the best of 1970s Pre-Pub Rockers!
Part 1

Much too much ink has been spilled on the subject of punk rock, freakbeat, mod, psych and underground music over the years — especially in the last five.

In the humble opinion of your scribe, these labels are merely a sign that the marketing bods have won. Bollocks, say I. It's all rock. That's right! We like the Tea Company AND Black Flag, Buffalo Springfield AND The Eyes. We like Mickey Newbury, The Monks, Poco AND the Cockney Rejects!!! (Whoa boy, let's not get TOTALLY carried away!! — RH)

Let's face it, it's very likely that most of my dear readers will tick the none-of-the-above box for at least some of the bands I like and write about. I've been gathering these primordial posers together for around 20 years. It's probably inevitable. But what do I care? I don't agree with much that Bobby Gillespie's ever said, but he was right about the lack of boogie in modern rock. And very few people have bothered to look into the good time boogie of 1970s pre-pub-rock.

I was talking with a young friend some years ago and he was speaking as if punk had always existed But I retorted that there was no punk before punk, at least, not as such (and, yes, I have read Lester Bangs and Stewart Home, so don't bother writing in. . . !!!). That led me to thinking about what came before it.

Naturally, it was pub rock and northern soul that sprang to mind. I haven't got the patience that northern soul requires, so I had a look at pub rock.

Even right in the middle of the most (self-)righteous musical year ever — I'm talking late-1976 to early 1977 here — there was no such thing as punk in most of the known world. Let alone where I came from.

"So what on earth did you lot do for kicks back then?" I hear massed voices asking in mooing tones from beneath asymmetric haircuts. Do I really have to go into it one more time? Surely everyone's read Julian Cope's "Head-On" by now.

Okay, it was like this...

Let me take you back for a gander at the hits, misses and long-gone-dug 12-bar grunts and wheezes from the old school. These are some of the results of half a life trawling through bargain bins, charity shops, and set sales.

"Doo-adda-doo-adda-doo"
Gimlet's tale

I first heard about Gimlet back in 1979, when I was making a living selling tapes of gigs I'd been to. (Mind you, it felt like I was dying on my arse at the time! — RH) My mate Tony gave me a C60, which boasted three whole tunes of theirs, among a load of other grease-stained nuggets. He'd been in possession of said item for a couple of years.

Gimlet hailed from Leamington Spa. They started in 1974, rising from the ashes of Torbett Longe's Measuring Bowl, a half-decent very-late-psych outfit that failed to record and certainly didn't stir the public imagination, even locally. Perhaps it was that name... Anyhow, I digress. Those three songs ("Please let me in", "Can I get into your heart?" and "Try to get inside your door") were the key to my interest in the hard rockin' bands of the mid-70s.

All of those three tunes have (still have — I'm listenin' to 'em now) the urge of The Troggs and a sheer, loose love of uptight boogaloo.

Everyone knows about Jesse Hector and Roogalator — and boy are they good — but for my money Gimlet have the bare-faced balls to boogie (bear balls?!?!), which few British acts have ever matched (as do other Rockhunter hard rockers: watch out for later issues!!). Think Small Faces, Tony Joe White, Sex Pistols (arguably the last of the best boogie bands). Man, I've gotta put out a CD of this stuff, and soon!!!

But the star to follow as far as Gimlet are concerned is the impossibly rare "Doo-adda-doo-adda-doo". Even the band haven't got copies!! In fact, I may have the only one in existence!!! But more of that later...

The First Ever Gimlet Interview

Undaunted by my failure to locate Colin Fogarty, Phil "Lenny" Burnham, or the mysterious "Kidda" (despite covering enough mileage to wear 50p-sized holes in my shoes), I sallied forth to run the rest of the blighters to ground. Needless to say (for you hold in your hands the evidence) I caught up with the other two band members.

Phil Arrow, Gimlet's lead guitar and founder member, still occasionally plays in pubs around his local area (he's now running a successful double-glazing business in Oxfordshire).

Speaking about the early days, he says: "The Measuring Bowl was a bit of a ragbag — an oddity. We were running around playing Motown covers, Quicksilver-style jams and one or two original numbers in the Hendrix mould, but we never gelled as such."

"Later on, like a lot of small groups in the 70s, we realised people wanted something a bit more gutsy than most of the studenty stuff around — something they could dance to — so we started stripping down some of our old tunes and chucking in some old rockers and blues numbers. You've got to realise that a lot of people just wanted to hear rock and roll — not Nick Drake."

Asked if their change of heart did them any good, Arrow says, "Let's put it this way, my mum never got that bungalow I promised her!"

Denny Wilson, bass guitar (now an estate agent in the Leamington Spa area) spoke on the phone and offered me a reflection on the whole experience. "I can't say with my hand on my heart that we changed the world," he reminisces, "but we had some laughs in Birmingham and London."

He continued: "I suppose people are more sophisticated now. Back then, all you had to do was pump out a Chuck Berry intro and you'd have the ladies backing up round the block."

A little bird tells me that there was an incident involving on-stage flashing. What happened there?

Denny: "One night in Birmingham, Col (Colin Fogarty) was doing his usual harp solo and broke into a rather impressive duck walk, but his strides couldn't take the strain and they ripped right open as he jumped up on the bass drum and waggled his arse to the crowd. Now, Col was always up for a bit, so he never wore pants. One minute there's an empty dance floor, the next thing there's half the birds in Brum cheering his goolies."

"He knew nothing about it, of course, because he was always half-pissed So we were trying to do a cover-up job as half the blokes at the dance were making up their minds about kicking our arses back to Leamington Spa. As it happens, they saw the funny side and shook our hands afterwards, so that was all right. There was other times we weren't so lucky, but that's life on the road."

What were your main influences? Phil: "We was all big on all the old rockers — the Vincents, the Richards, the Cochrans and so on — that was my first love in music. And we all loved Big Brother, Quicksilver, Motown, Hendrix — that style of thing. All the Yank psychedelia, maaan."

Halfway through talking to Phil I caused some consternation when I opened up my bag of tricks and showed him my cassette copy of the 3-song demo from 1975. He even more amazed when I revealed an original, pristine(-ish) one-sided acetate of the blood-racing, rock-a-rollin', and totally unknown, "Doo-adda-doo-adda-doo".

Phil: "I'd like to know how you got one of those. I never even got a copy."

Sensing a mutiny in my interviewee, I hastily promised him multiple copies in any format he desired.

RH: Was there any interest following the demo sessions.

"No," Phil sighs, "It was all self-produced We were putting down a tough Doo-Wop bop at that time. We had a few sniffs, but Lenny buggered off just as the demo was doing the rounds."

"Easily our best tune, that one," Denny opines. "It took 5 months to get a replacement, what with us trying to hold down jobs and that. By the time Kidda arrived it was all over bar the shouting."

RH: Any regrets?

Phil: "No. None. We did our bit. You can't rock forever. Look at that prat Jagger! Mind you, I can still fill a pair of jeans, if you know what I mean."

With that scary thought boring into my synapses, I took my leave of Gimlet and high-tailed it home by National Express, before the precious acetate was wrenched from my clammy grasp.

GIMLET PERSONNEL

Phil Arrow — Lead Guitar/ Vocals
Denny Wilson — Bass Guitar/ Vocals
Phil "Lenny" Burnham — Drums (1974-1975)
"Kidda"—Drums (1975-1976)
Colin Fogarty — Guitar/Vocals/Harp

GIMLET DISCOGRAPHY

- Unreleased demo, May 1975
  "Please let me in" (Arrow/Fogarty)
  "Can I get into your heart?" (Arrow/Fogarty)
  "Try to get inside your door" (Fogarty/Arrow)
- Acetate, November 1975,
  "Doo-adda-doo-adda-doo"
  (Arrow/Fogarty/Lent/Wilson)

EDITORIAL

I've been e-mailed with some sage advice about producing a fanzine. Without wishing to sound rude, I'd like to cordially invite my correspondent to roll this issue of Rockhunter into a neat tube and insert it up his interfering anus!!!

I go to a lot of time and effort doing all this. And why no pictures? Listen. You do it your way and I'll do it mine!!!

All the best.
Your Editor

NEXT TIME

The next issue will be a stop-gap issue, featuring some modern bands (whoa, boy!) and reviews of some new (-ish) comps.

6

October 2003

Including: Brown Stripes, Lost Sounds of The Grympen Myre and English Regional Punk

Modern News

Speaking of the awkward squad, another reprehensible bunch of reprobates from the Brighton area have come to my attention in the past months since my last foray into the murky world of the magazine media.

The Brown Stripes have been raising some eyebrows with their particularly twisted version of the anti-bass movement in indie-rock. This uncle and niece combo is currently in talks with a large record company (it sez 'ere). Good for them. If you want to release large records, go to a large record company!!

This is not the first Brighton band to court the majors over the years, and I suspect it will not be the last, given the amount of talentless Pop Idol-fodder down-shifting from London in search of a vanished Bohemia. I can't stand 'em!! (More spleen vented on that in later issues, I'm sure!!!).

As well as the obvious spoof reference, which will win them few friends in the fashion-hungry world of indie-garage, the Brown Stripes seem to be heading on a crash course with the new moral militia. (Although they are not hurtling towards that morass as fast as that other bunch of Sussex scallywags, Speedophile). Their whole schtick is based on a white trash ethic, but they're not doing it fashionista style.

The picture accompanying their demo is pretty ugly. It looks like The Cardiacs auditioning for a Phoenix Nights talent showcase. I'm not kidding. These people look seriously nuts.

Sonya (guitar) and Ian (guitar) have produced a cassette featuring three of their current tunes: (1) "Pink Straw", (2) "My Owl" and (3) "Midnight Feast". All songs are done in classic Cramps style, with two guitars wailing and a bluesy shout over the top.

I like the last tune best, the first two being a bit too straight out of the my first garage band textbook. And I've heard of lot of that sort of stuff in my time. Er, where was I? "Midnight Feast" is basically, "When The Levee Breaks" crossed with "Moulty", and it's all the better for those references worn on the sleeve. I've not heard a better slow blues builder for some time, and that's some praise, believe me!

However, the big question mark is, I'm not sure if I'm being taken for a ride by these people. It's possible that this is the same crew that almost scammed me in the summer of 2001 with a creditable CD (with authentic crackles and tape hiss) purporting to emerge from late-1969/early-1970 by an outfit called The Brown Acid.

Whatever their vintage, I still reckon The Brown Acid could have made the grade with a couple of their tunes. The excellent "Sweet Drunken Ladies" could have easily graced The Darkness's set. I presume they've gone the way of all flesh, since the last in a series of increasingly frantic and deranged press releases told of their frustration with music business bread-heads and their imminent demise.

Anyhow, it wouldn't be the first time I've been had. (And that's another in a long series of long, long stories! — RH)

It'll be interesting to see whether the Brown Stripes make it out of the garage, but if they do, you better believe I'll be there.

LIVELY ONES

I got quite a haul the other week. A mate of mine acquired (no names, no pack drill!!) a number of ultra-rare acetates. Effendi, I make special price for you, my friend!!! Some I knew, but most were a complete mystery.

One, however, was a mystery wrapped in an enigma that had then been wrapped in bacon and roasted with all the trimmings. It was "Offerings In The Time of Mind" b/w "Ancient Village" by The Grympen Myre. I'm not often surprised any more, after years and years of trolling around musty shops and back rooms. But on this occasion I was genuinely intrigued. What was this unknown disc doing in the hands of my mate?

I know that things still turn up, but I've only been lucky enough to find a handful of complete unknown unknowns in 30 odd years of collecting (and some were very odd indeed, believe you me!!). And here was my old mucker with a wheelbarrow load!!! The thot plickens.

Anyway, I took said treasure home and gave it a spin and I was totally amazed. Far from being a wet, soft-sike nightmare, as I'd suspected, The Myre lay down a hell of a sound. Somewhere between Jason Crest and Black Sabbath, if you can get with that...

The A-side has all the hallmarks of great heavy psych, which, its no secret, is entirely my bag. Clanging bell-like guitars give way to a plump, rolling ascendant bass line.

There's something holy and, at the same time, unholy, about the way this tune grabs you with whimsy and then bites yer hands with total riff-based heaven. However, a question mark hangs over the flip. Coming on like The Attack, or The Game, this is a real oddity, because the arrangement and ampage, to my ears, is totally early-mid 70s.

For a comparison, think Flintlock riding shotgun for Love. There you go. No idea about this one. The guitars are fresh and un-muddled, but the drums are out of a totally different beat era.

That's what I love about this game. You never know what you'll turn up. (Apologies for coming all over Forrest Gump!). The others I did not hear, but I've paid a deposit on 3 of them. So hopefully, I'll hear some knockout sounds and knock out a couple of reviews in the next ish.

More about my surprise new finds later on!!!

LOCKED AWAY FOR A MILLION YEARS

As I write this I'm listening to a great new comp received the other day from a new outfit in Psych Town. They're called Woollen Records and they're based on the south coast, according to the not-very-helpful info on the sleeve!!

Don't know about you, but I wholly approve of the idea of woollen records. They'd be easier to store and you'd only need a knitting needle to play them. Mind you, you'd have to watch out for moth. I digress!

This fledgling outfit's latest waxing is titled "Locked Away For A Million Years: English Regional Punk, 1963-1980". Taking, I presume, Tim Warren's (Mr. Back From The Grave's) personal style to heart, Thee guys (girls??!!) at Woollen (This guy? This girl, even? — RH) have taken a slightly more human approach to the usually stodgy comp game and come up with the intriguing notion of banging all their favourites on a long-player.

This intriguing approach gives us all a peek inside their wigged-out noggins and vast collections with number 4 (or, to give it it's proper reference, Vol. IV) in their Locked Away series. And very generous too, say I.

With the great sweep of time taken in in this comp, you can really see some interesting connections emerging. The big question is, how the hell did I miss the first three in the series? Bah!

The idea of sorting out the English scene into regions is also an intriguing one. Long since accepted as a way of getting to grips with the US scene, it's high time that some one did the same for the UK, which had tremendous variations throughout during the 60s onwards.

If you're a coincidence freak, then the following story should send you into orbit, my wheezy freak-bothering friend! What should I find on Side Two, Band One? The Grympen Myre B-side!! I kid you not.

When you've been collecting, swapping and hunting around for as long as I have, you get to realise that this is a very small world. But even I was surprised by the inclusion of The Mighty Myre on this new comp. Seems like the Woollen people have a yen for the same kind of warped vinyl as me.

The starters on each side are genuine unknown diamonds. Side One kicks off with "Your Carriage Awaits", a weird psych ballad from Christopher Eager (think the less successful alter-ego of Thane Russall!!!). There's fuzz lines, big fluffy bass and crescendo drumming galore.

I also really like The Christmas Game's "Locked Away For A Million Years" — from which the whole series gets its name — which to my mind is a negative answer song to The Mirror's "Faster Than Light".

Most of the other tunes are a pretty hit-and-miss bunch, in my opinion. And all of the late-punk offerings eat considerable amounts of doo-doo, in my humble opinion. It still has to be said that this compilation is the way forward, unless comps are to become a totally redundant form.

But if you like your rhythm bluesy and your beat freaky, there's plenty of feedback, howling cats, and so forth, to keep you satisfied.

My only complaint about this otherwise utterly beaterly product is that despite Woollens south coast location, there's not a sausage — nada, if you will — by bands from that part of the world. Methinks they should have contacted a certain interested party...

The other Woollen LP is a very strange proposition indeed. It's a live performance from 1971 by a band called The Druid College. The sound quality is appalling and the songs are long, early-prog-like rambles with riffy interludes reminiscent of Interstellar-vintage Floyd, or Quicksilver.

I can't really recommend this one with my hand on my heart, psych fans, but their riff-heavy stylings have got to get them some attention in Collector-land.

Editorial

No time this time. Maybe next time!!

All the time.

Your Editor

Next Time

OK!! I know you 'orrible lot are still waitin for Fen and Devon punk, psych and heavy boogiosity, but gimme a break, I"m getting there!!!

Late 2006 edit

I've recently heard that a bunch of ne'er-do-wells is doing the rounds as The Brown Stripes in the pubs of Brighton. I hasten to add that this not the same band as the one I leapt up to champion even before their first gig. Notwithstanding (Just what does that word mean? — RH) the fact that my Brown Stripes (an unforgettable image, to be sure!!! — Picture — RH) are defunct, I stress that the two bands are as different as one cheese is from another.

And little surprise that Speedophile didn't make it to the end. Rumour has it they were stoned to death by a mob searching for a decent tune. C'est la vie.

Now then,

Your Editor

7

Halloween Special
October 2003

It's only one letter away from "Cockhunter" — but this organ does not suck!

Greasers Doin' The Boogie
The Best Of 1970s Pre-Pub Rockers!
Part 2

There are those who sing the praises of the likes of Eggs Over Easy and those who prefer the gangland punk boogie of The Count Bishops. I guess at this stage I should run up my flag and admit to being somewhere in the middle ground — or should I say the no-mans land? — of the hard rock debate.

I never set any store by the panacea of punk, and I certainly don't wan't to hitch my pony to the tenderfoot wagons of the new hard rock, as personified by the likes of The Darkness.

Okay, so Justin and the boys are raising Cain in a music biz fascinated, for the nth time in a generation, by the sound of actual guitars. And let us not forget that they've admitted theyre from the Lowestoft area!!

But let's face it, the only thing that's gonna get us the hell outta this current rockin' crisis is knowing where we come from and where were going. Those who forget their rock are doomed to repeat it.

Cos we sure as heck ain't gonna get any clues from a dirty business that's currently selling us the past as new. I digress, but when don't I?

The Past in Traction

In this, the second part of an occasional series, we focus on Traction, one of my personal favourite bands, and the epitome of the power trio, to boot. They packed a whole world of insane riffola into their one single, "You Giaconda, Me Da Vinci", released in 1974. It's chock full of the kinda funk they should put on prescription. And they pipped Jesse Hectors fabulous Gorillas to the recording post!!

Even their biggest fan would have to admit that Traction didn't exactly set the world alight. With a singleton 45 to their name, they missed success by a country mile. But their rowdy blues guaranteed them a place in the record pile on the floor in my flat!! (As we speak, I bet they're quitting work and buying new guitars!! — RH)

I caught Andy Rowe (bass/vocals) at a bad time, but he kindly agreed to answer a few questions and say a few words about his time in Traction. And here he is, in his own words:

Andy: Probably only a couple of people remember us, cos we never really did much outside Huddersfield. But 10 out of 10 for tracking me down, though!

Traction happened because me and Alan wanted to carry on playing after our old band, Treacle, called it a day. We were basically playing dance halls and so on, with a set of mainly old soul numbers.

You'll laugh at this, but we never had a name for that one, and we called it Treacle for a laugh, because that's what it felt like — wading through the same old soddin' tunes night after night!

Basically, we'd all got traditionally pissed on Christmas Eve and met up around closing time in Holmfirth, of all places. We had a phase going to country pubs! Me and Alan were at a loose end. Laurie had been knocking around for years. We knew him from seeing him socially and knew he played, but that was it.

Funnily, enough, that night he was doing his best Noel Redding impersonation in a pick-up band, otherwise me and Alan would never have broached the subject with him. It all just blossomed from there.

RH: And before that?

Andy: That would be about 71 to 73 — so we're now going back to 67. Phew, that's dating me! Well, around that time I was playing in a couple of bands. There was Prausutagus — he was Boadiccea's husband, although she's actually pronounced Boodika, as in B.O.O.D.I.K.A (I actually knew that!! — RH Woad), 6:30, Nature's Man. I was always into my history — long before Time Team!!

RH: I've not heard about 6:30.

Andy: That was my brainchild. We used to do covers mainly. But we had a couple of good originals. I started it in 68. We pissed all over most of the local competition. Oh, 6:30 was the time I had to get up and got to work — usually after a heavy night being heavy!!!

Those are the ones I can remember. Before that it was The Charioteers, from about 62 to 66. (Later, in 1969, as Pharoahs Chariot, but without Andy, they'd release "Land Over Sky" b/w "Within My Sight And Sound" — RH) I've got a tape of some of that stuff somewhere.

RH: I'd really like to hear that. How did the single come about?

Andy: A lad we knew a bloke who owned a local record shop who fancied getting into the business. So, the usual arrangements were made, and we all got in the van, bombed off to Sheffield and recorded a demo.

Obviously, as you know, there was no real interest from the London crowd. They reckoned we were too raw for the market at that time. So we decided to let Graeme at the shop do it. He put it out on Garden Gate, his own label. He'd just got a new place with his missis and was really proud with the garden. Plonker. Anyway, that's all past history.

RH: I've heard that the live act was something else.

Andy: We used to put a lot of work into getting the right sound. We went into attack mode right from the off. And we weren't a pretty bunch, either. A journalist on the Daily Examiner once described us as less outta sight, more building site!!!

And that was that. DIY beckoned, and he was off!!

Traction Personnel

Andy Rowe — Bass/Vocals
Laurie Cordon — Bass/Vocals
Alan Northolt — Drums

Traction Discography

- Garden Gate Records, 7 single, 1974 "You Giaconda, Me Da Vinci" (Rowe/Cordon) "Later, Later" (Rowe)
- Home-recording, 1974 (cassette supplied by Andy Rowe) "Sue Can Do It" (Unknown)

Letters To God?

Just opened a package that's worthy of mention in this august organ. Your man from Other Fucker Records has bunged me a new re-issue CD, Letters To God? Vol. I, from his ever-increasing stable of, er, re-issue CDs. Strictly for those in the know. For they are not exactly legal. Nor are they exactly not illegal. If you know what I mean. (And if you do know what I mean, let me know. I'd be eternally great!! — RH)

Still ploughing their lonely furrow (Ouch! They really should get out more!! — RH) in the minefield of shoddy moddy psych acetates, OFR have, as usual, dug up some mouldy old gems and some utter toss (sorry fellas!). But that's the deal with comps, right?

Totally the best track is "Helmet, Sword and Shield" by the Bronze Age Treasure, a blazing burial mound of pre-prog treasure, evoking the ghosts of Sutton Hoo, Beowulf, trans-European prehistory, ley lines, revisionist archaeology and the little people. OK, so I made that up. But what the f***? To my cloth ears, this is as good as it gets with recorded sound — as long as you like Him and The Others, the Buff Medways, ect., ect.

No room to mention any more. Look out for a fuller round-up next time

Editorial — Backtrackin'

I've been asked to provide a full track listing for Woollen Records' "Locked Away For A Million Years, Vol. IV" (see Issue Six). Always ready and willing to oblige — but unable this time due to no room, as usual.

Maybe next time!!

Your Editor.

P.S. And no, there's no pumpkins. The horror's in the sound!!

Stripey News Flash

Last month's ish mentioned a cockamamie outfit called the Brown Stripes. Anyway, it turns out that Sonya is not really Ian's niece. Phew! I was getting a bit worried there... But apparently she is a bit special needs (it sez 'ere). Oh gawd!!!

Next Time

Interview and retrospective on Suffolk heaviosity heroes Ginger Tom. Plus more ace reviews of comps that have passed through my eager mitts. But you'll have to wait for the full sad and sorry tale of our non-interview with The State of Mickey and Tommy.

Soon you'll be nuzzling round my swill bin for more treats, including Fen and Devonian punk, psych and heavy, a bumper Xmas rarities extravaganza, etc. There's only so much a man can do. Meanwhile, stick around for more hard rockin' boogie action. XXXXX

8

NOVEMBER 2003

"The weight of the one is the weight of the whole" — Gene Clark

MORE NEW BRIGHTON STUFF

Out on Cormorant later this month, I recommend you sell your shoes or your mum's jewellery, or both, and get these two discs from Borderline immediately: The Shades of Meaning, "Back In The Day" b/w "When You Know You're Going To Be Alright" & The Creeping Past, "The Creeping Past" b/w Threshold People, "No Place".

The Shades of Meaning are a strange proposition indeed. The A sounds like The Outsiders, or Wings, tackling a Choir-style melodic folker. It's a little bit predictable — but all the better for it, say I!! The flip is a bizarre, but superior, cheerful-yet-moody Meek-style rocker, with a pounding beat, strident bass-line and a chorus not a million miles away from The Jam's "Something's Gone". (No, I do not mean Weller's wankers!! See Pebbles 9 for enlightenment. — RH)

The 2nd Cormorant 45 is a split single (haven't seen one of these rare beasts for a while — RH) featuring two groups trying to outdo each other in the last-garage-band Derby.

The eponymous "The Creeping Past" is a Lovecraftian monstrosity with so many hooks you could go line-fishing for endangered piscine species and still catch a dozen innocent dolphins!!! The words are a hoot, too. Imagine an underwater village off the shore of Hove, where an Elder Groop lurks waiting to attack unbelieving land-lubber bands every 30 years or so. Woo-oo-oooo!! Truly unsettlingly weird stuff!!

"No Place" by the Threshold People is somewhat more traditional. It's a pretty standard folk-rocker with a hook reminiscent of The One-Way Streets' "Peanut Butter" (Reminiscent?! It's the goddam same!! — RH) and a middle-eight straight outta the beery wastes of Fratland.

The main thing that gets this side a mention in dispatches is that it's a message song about how poor old Brighton's being sold, like Jack's cow at market, or a premier division footballers arse. The only thing is, there's not even any magic beans on offer in return — and no way to kill the evil giant!! So fuck the council for their conjuring/marketing tricks. (BHC! BHC! You're full of shit, shit, shit, shit, shit!! — RH, with apologies to Menace.) And thanks a bunch to the Threshold People for getting me riled up. I'll now have to spend at least two hours shouting at the box before trudging up the wooden hill to my special technicolour dreams — bah!!!

READERS' WIRES

I've been getting some far-out e-mails!! In fact, some of the stuff I've been sent is so out-there it's gone round and come back in for tea before going out to play for a couple of hours before bedtime!!

Here's one I really like — it's an excerpt from Jurgen Maas's recent interview with the legendary fiddler and rock sessioneer Clem "Oakie" Doakes.

Okay, well, back in 1965 me and Bobby Underwood [banjoist — better known for his picking for Good n Sweet] had a little bluegrass band called the Greensboro Bluegrass Pickers.

We played every week at Ralph's. [The Suntime Bowling Alley, Greensboro, owned and run by Ralph Trimmer]. Things were pretty good, but sometimes we complained that no one could hear us over the noise of the balls and the pins. See, in those days bowling alleys didn't have real good sound. But that's a money gig and no other place would let two guys sit and pick a session — except in the car park.

Things were steady enough for us to put out a couple of 45s over the years. [The best are arguably "Pickin' a Tune" b/w "Hells Teeth", Tall Tree, TT2212, 1967 and the slightly controversial "Dance on the Red Man" b/w "Our Land, Our Land". Both releases are archived on Vanguard's fine tribute LP, Bowling Alley Folk, VAN2643].

We were held back by an initial lack of success, but then hard rock came down the pike. We knew those guys were comin down to check us out most times we played. One night someone told us that Ted Nugent was bowling in aisle 19 — giving him a bird's eye view of my fretting hand. So I flipped him the bird! I guess it was time for us to move on.

And move on he did. Clem's searing fiddle licks and explosive vamping technique adapted well to psych-rock guitar, as heard on tracks like the exceptional "Pale in the Morning" by Greensboro also-rans the Lost Dawgs [check out the download on www.totallyunheardof.com].

When the 70s really got underway around 1974, Clem's unusual musical pedigree and ability to play 16 notes per second placed him in high demand with the hard rock — and later the heavy metal — fraternity.

It was one foot in the barnyard and one in the stadium for goin on 15 years! I played with everyone — Warrant, Ratt, you name it. There's a lot between bluegrass and hard rock — the speed and attitude.

These days Clem's traded the widdle back for the fiddle and currently fronts tribute band Ban-Jovi. He gets the last word — which is the way he likes it.

I can't say I'm their biggest fan, but once I thought of the name I couldn't think of nothing else. It's a good show. We do a traditional gospel version of "Living on a Prayer" as the closer. We even play back in the bowling alley — though it's a goddam corporate franchise now. But at least they got a P.A.

[Jurgen's website, Totallyunheardof.com, is currently under construction.]

OK, bluegrass isn't exactly my bag — although the sinister Uncle Dave Macon is ace and I would give my prize Wimple Winch 45s for a time machine ride to see Clarence White do his amazing bendy thing. But I was stunned to see a mention of Lost Dawgs!! (And by the way, if anyone knows what a widdle is, please mail me!! — RH)

For the uninitiated, the Lost Dawgs make Quicksilver sound like The Smiths — and I love 'em!! Their sole 45, "Pale in The Morning" b/w "Where D'You Get Your Whiskey?" was released in 1968. You ain't likely to have heard it, folks, so don't write tellin' me how much you dig it!!

The A is amazing — a howlin', wailin' trip!! What can I say? I've gotta do a piece on these guys sometime. The flip is based on an old-time bluegrass number, "I Get My Whiskey From Rockingham". Like Quicksilver, the Dawgs take the blues for a good ole Louisiana hay-ride — dragging it through town behind a pony, before coshing it, stealing its dinner money, rolling it in a rug and pushing it out of a moving vehicle outside its own front door!!!

Edit: Then, some time later, Hayseed Dixie come along and fulfil the promise of Jurgen's moist dream. Well I never. Although his website never did get beyond construction stage. I wonder where he went. Same place as me, I guess. Ulp!!!!

Dirty Burds
Sabotage Club, Brighton, October

I've got to admit I went along to see this lot under false pretences — but mine, not theirs, I hasten to add!! I remembered an all-girl outfit from way back in the 90s called The Budget Girls and, from the description of the Burds, I thought it was them and went by mistake! My old memory certainly ain't what it was!!

Anyway, back to the matter in hand. So what if the Dirty Burds are not exactly spring chickens?! (In fact, a little bird — who may or may not be dirty — tells me they're well past spring and already into late summer!! — RH) As long as bands are ready and willing to bring back the boogie and ditch the lifestyle bollocks, I shall always be there to raise a glass and tip my hat to 'em — male or female.

The Burds ditch the stoopid attitude posturing and get down to chooglin' along with their own brand of meat-and-two-veg hard rockin boogie!! And they do a spiffing cover version of the Real Kids' "Do The Boob" to boot!! Go see 'em soon, you 'orrible lot!!

Yoiks!! Girls who know about Real Kids LP tracks??! Where do they hang out? I guess I've wasted my life. Maybe I should stay away from record fairs and blokes who are more interested in Misfits or VU bootlegs than scoring with super-looking ladies!? (Watch out, boys!! It could happen to you too!! — RH).

More Words From The Past

As well as getting showered with abuse (see below), I've also received some genuine queries about what I'm doing here. A lot of people have asked what happened to the first three issues.

Rockhunter the magazine started back in June 1992 when issue No.1 was thrust rudely in the face of the general public. March 1994 saw the unleashing of No.2, and No.3 limped off the press in June 1996.

For the uninitiated, these were glossy 20-30 page mags with pics. They were pretty expensive to do. And basically, I've got none left and no money to re-print, even if I wanted too. So, as Jimmy Cliff said, that's the way life goes — but tomorrow never knows.

It might be worth checking out the usual London shops, because they may get some in second-hand very occasionally. But it was mainly a Brighton thing — and Brighton may as well have been the moon in the dark days before New Labour, chilling out in public and the place-to-fucking-be (Gah!! — RH)

Even Slim Chance, the legendary promoter at the St Johns Tavern, Archway, had his work cut out getting his hip London and Home Counties regulars to make it down to the BN area for 60s-scene gigs and rekkid hops in the early to mid-90s.

Of course, it's all changed now. These days you can't move for urban mods, greasy clods, arseholes, down-sizers and shape-shifters, asymmetric stary girls — and general hair don'ts—ninnies, twerps, twits, twats, and feebs and berks of the first water.

I've put out an APB on common sense! ... Calling all cars!! Calling all cars!! ... fetch me another bottle of Talisker ... mummy!! ... aaaaaarrrrrrggggggh!!!

Rory McGrath Is An Absolute Cunt

In addition to getting loads of e-mails from assorted nutters and ne'er-do-wells, I've also had the usual rash of nasty buggers. The worse I've seen in the past two months has described me as, and I quote, "doing for rock n roll what Rory McGrath's done for cable TV and popular culture in general."

What can I say? I'm cut to the quick to be compared to that filthy, unfunny sack of shit. Only last week I was agog to see the dickhead on BBC2s Grumpy Old Men, complaining about how crappy and vacuous everything is these days, especially the popular media.

Now, I've invested a considerable amount of time in checking out the moral abyss of the popular media (daytime telly branch), and I have to say that this is pretty rich coming from the man who once hosted a morning show on a local cable TV channel in Cambridge devoted — as far as I could see — to him getting drunk on cocktails and embarrassing the unpaid unfortunates around him, especially the young women. The cunt.

Love
Your Editor XXXXX

9

Dec 2003 / Jan 2004

"I've lost all my pride. / I've been through paradise and out the other side. / With no one to guide me, / Torn apart by a fiery wheel inside me." — West Coast Pop Art

Greasers Doin' The Boogie
The Best of 1970s Pre-Pub Rockers!
Part 3

Say the words Ginger Tom to most people in the Bury St Edmunds area these days and you'll get a shrug and a funny look. But it was a different story back in the mid-70s, when the dance halls were being torn up by a bunch of Suffolk renegade rockers.

I first encountered the Ginger Tom sound in early 1978 at roughly the same time I was getting bored of clocking so-called punk rock bands that only a few months previously had been doin the hand-jive boogie with the best of 'em. You know who I mean — previously — flared-up geezers like The Vibrators, and the rest. I was a contrary old sod even then, so just as the provinces were beginning to get it on to the new-style beat-boom bands, I was time-tunnelling back to the roots of rock.

In the January I found a copy of the Wild Angels LP, Live at the Revolution and was getting off on their tough bop. By the March I had given up on the so-called new wave. By the April I was galvanised in my choice after being given a cassette featuring various unknown English rockers by a bloke I met at a record fair in Norwich. So if you're reading this, mate, thanks — and the rest of you 'orrible lot now know who to blame!!

Up until hearing the hoary old rockers contained therein that cassette, I'd thought that Johnny Kidd and the Pirates were the livin' end of British rock 'n' roll. How wrong was I, eh? (Er, any chance of actually getting to the matter in hand? — Hopeful RH)

Among the many not-so-memorable names on that fateful tape was Ginger Tom. Well, that was it for me. The Tom's huge-sounding "Can It Be True", a grinding barrage of hate-you, filthy dirty bastard boogie, was all the nudge I needed to hurl myself off the waggon and dive right back into the hard rock I'd dodged since hearing the Sex Pistols for the first time.

The Pistols attracted me up the garden path with their slinky, boogie-heavy take on sleazebag punk rock. Unfortunately, the aftermath of their trawl through the self-satisfied, smug little London of the mid-70s seemed to lead straight back to the art school, rather than the boozer via the record shop, which is the route I favoured at the time. I've no problem with art schools, it's just that I'm full of envious hatred for something I never had. Anyway, for what it's worth, that, my friends, is how I fell out of love with the big idea of 70s punk.

I was horrified to discover that none of the so-called experts had ever heard of this ace new outfit I'd just come across called Ginger Tom. I found out then that ignorance is the Achilles Heel of the record collector — they never want to admit they don't know something. (Blimey, this is becoming a memoir, lemme outta here!!! — RH)

Oh, Just Get On With It!

So, to cut a short story long, suffice it to say it took me some years to track down more of the Gingers' output, but track it down I certainly did (see my exclusive and exhaustive discography at the end of this feature)!! And that's not all. Just a couple of months ago I managed to get in touch with their main man Dave Bacon — Ginger

Tom hisself — the man for whom the group hath been named.

Boy was he surprised to get a Tom-related phone call after all those years!! I blagged an exclusive interview with him for this ish.

But enough of this! I hear you sob impatiently!! So, without further ado, ladies and gentlemen, I present to you, for one night only, the majestic, raw, and dare I say slightly frightening, GINGER TOM!!!! May God have mercy on our souls.

Ginger, You're Barmy!

Dave Bacon now lives in a very nice property in Cavenham, a quiet little village 5 miles west of the middle of nowhere. He divides his time between here and the Algarve.

Anyway, picture two middle-aged men drinking cans of lager in the sunshine in an idyllic rural setting...

RH: Could you tell me a bit about how you started playing?

Dave "Ginger Tom" Bacon: The main thing to remember is, none of us never had any illusions about playing in a band, we basically wanted to have a laugh, get laid, and rip it up a bit. At no time did any of us sit down and say, I'll do this and you do that. All we did was get some guitars and that, then get it together a couple of nights a week after work. It's as simple as that.

RH: And your first gig?

GT: My first ever gig was playing in a band with some mates at a party in Tuddenham. We rocked the joint with two little old guitar amps.

RH: For the connoisseurs of guitars, amps and such, what sort of gear were you using?

GT: Let me see. I had a Fenton Weil six-string, Rich [Rich Andrews, rhythm guitar] had a proper Fender Stratocaster, lucky bastard — the first one in Bury, as far as I'm aware. He worked for the GPO as an electrician or something, so say no more. At that time Barry would have been using a little Hofner bass, one of those 3/4-size-looking things. I can't remember what drum set Bernie [Bernie Leggett, drums] had during the Tom years, but it would have been a decent one, cos his mum and dad weren't short of a few bob.

As for amps, I had a Watkins something-or-other, and Rich had a Selmer Treble n Bass, which the bass had to go through as well. And we bunged the vocal mike through a homemade amp and cab we borrowed off a mate. I'll admit to failing to blow the roof off the joint!

RH: What were you called then?

GT: Er, that would've been The Chocolate Fire. We were great, did a bit of Cheer, Buddy Holly, Arthur Brown, a bit of The Seeds, a bit of this and a bit of that.

The girls loved it, though, and that was that main point of the whole thing. We'd obviously laid on a load of booze, which helped.

RH: How old were you when you first started playing?

GT: I was 16, but by the time I'd started Ginger Tom I was 19.

RH: And the others?

GT: As for the others in the Tom, Rich was 21, Barry was 20, and Bernie was just 17. He was a shit-hot drummer though.

RH: When did Ginger Tom start?

GT: That would've been around 1973, in the January, I seem to remember. New year, new start, and all that.

RH: And how did things kick off?

GT: Well, I hadn't played for a few months and I bumped into Rich and Leggy [Bernie Leggett's nickname]. They were in a dance-band kind of outfit called The Magic Lantern Band.

Rich was a right old boy, I can tell you, always running around. In his prime no woman could resist him. I wish I'd bottled it and sold it. We could've made a fortune.

Anyway, the money from the dances was good, but the boys had got a bit bored doing the same old crap night after night. One night we ended up going for a drink or eight and decided there and then to form a band.

RH: On a different tack, and without wanting to sound rude, it's pretty obvious how you got the nickname!

GT: Yeah, it's fair to say! It never bothered me, all the ginger stuff you used to get at school. I'm proud of what

I've done with my life, what I've achieved and, basically, who I am.

I had a whale of a time as a kid, playing in bands, getting my end away, and that. Christ, I hope my old lady don't read that!! Well, she knows what I was like.

RH: When did you decide on the name?

GT: Same night as the band started. It started out as a joke, but it just stuck.

RH: We you rehearsing for long?

GT: Well, no more than a couple of months, then we were out playing. BANG! Just like that. So we were a going concern almost from the off.

RH: Where was your first gig as Ginger Tom?

GT: Pass. But I remember a very early one at a birthday party in Thetford, a friend of a friend. We thought we'd stand a better chance if the audience was half pissed. Went down a storm, though.

RH: Most local scenes are fairly competitive. Who were your main rivals at the time?

GT: Well, there weren't really anyone doing the kind of thing we were doing, you know, all the running around the audience, geeing them up and that. But there was a few really good rock bands doing the rounds, like Lead Pencil, they were tight. Finesse, Marsh Grass.

Actually, thinking back, there was quite a few, I suppose, but most of them were doing covers. I suppose there was always a bit of competition, but never any aggro as such. The difference with us was that we were mostly doing our own tunes.

RH: How come you never got wider recognition outside your own area if you were doing something so different? Did you not get the breaks you deserved?

GT: I wouldn't say that, exactly. The thing is, we never really felt the need to do showcase gigs and the like. I don't even like London, so why would I want to spend my time chatting up a load of ponces up there? As I remember it, I think we were all pretty happy just knocking about playing here and there.

We all had jobs, you see, apart from Leggy. I can't even remember now what he did. Anyway, he was the best drummer I'd ever seen at the time. Apparently, he went on to do session work with the likes of Jona Lewie, Linton Kwesi Johnson, and Kate Bush. (It's all true, —RH) Apart from him, we all knew none of us was going set the world on fire as players. You've got to remember we all had jobs and were making a load of extra money as such when we did a concert.

RH: It's unusual to hear someone who made such great sounds that went pretty much unnoticed not being bitter about it.

GT: That's me all over.

RH: Could you tell me a bit about where you played in the local area?

GT: There was the place they did the folk club in Bury, can't remember its name now. Basically, we played all over the place in Cambridge, Norwich, and, well, loads of places, really. We were never short of a place to play. Trouble was, we weren't often asked back.

RH: Really? Okay, so your stuff was a bit near at times, I'm talking about the famous "On Your Knees" routine you used to do for encores. But I'd have thought that it would have gone down a storm out of the sticks. Did you never play in London?

GT: Yeah, well, we did some pub gigs around London in our later period. At that time everyone wanted to get a bit of rockin', to coin a phrase. There was Dr Feelgood, who were basically my heroes for a while, and Brinsley Schwartz, then there was Ducks Deluxe, and the rest. We never played with them, though. Because of travelling time we were limited to playing more in North London, around your Camdens and Finsbury Parks, that style of thing. I do regret that now, you know, not gigging more down there.

Ah, now, that whole "On Your Knees" tune only started as a bet. These days birds are queuing up for the same treatment by male strippers. Mind you, they're a damn sight better looking than we were!!! Anyway, least said, soonest mended I think!!

RH: You were telling me earlier about the records. The Tom was quite unusual because you got your own records pressed up. How did you come to the decision to be a DIY band rather than disappear in the industry sausage machine? And — dare I say it? — did you sell any discs?

GT: Oh, yeah. I suppose we were something of an oddity in terms of attitude. Like I said, we had no real idea of hitting it big, Mind you, I'd have jumped at the chance if any money had actually come our way!

The long and the short of it is that we did the records ourselves. We used to sell them in a few local shops, and then at our concerts. We sold quite a few. Looking back, it was a laugh more than anything else. You know, actually getting a record out was all we wanted to do.

RH: Everyone normally thinks that independent labels and bands doing their own thing came about during the punk rock explosion.

GT: Well, I suppose you could say we were punk rockers before our time. No, there was always bands chancing their arm all over the place. The thing is, we all loved the music and we just wanted to have something to call our own, if you know what I mean. You know, something to put next to all our favourite singles wed bought over the years.

RH: I've got to say that at least two of the single tracks "Can It Be True?" and "Memphis, Suffolk" are world-class numbers. Not to mention my personal favourite, "All Right My Woman", a bluesy rockin' revelation. I'm surprised the Tom aren't considered a classic pub rock act.

GT: I could get to like you, boy!! Yeah, well, the thing is, we never distributed them. There was no way we could sell them in shops outside the local area, because one knew who we were, did they? Like I said, we sold quite a few when we played, but there was no way we were going to hit the big time selling 10 here and half a dozen there. Of course, by the time Chiswick and that were doing their thing, it was a whole different ball game, but of course by then we were old history.

And that, dear readers, is where my tapes ran out!! Anyway, Dave had already broken out the Stellas and, not to put too fine a point on it, we got pissed, so there wasn't much in the way of coherence after this point anyway!!

Ginger Tom Personnel

Dave "Ginger Tom" Bacon — Lead guitar, vocals
Barry Kett — Bass guitar, backing vocals
Rich Andrews — Rhythm guitar, backing vocals
Bernie "Leggy" Leggett — Drums, backing vocals

Ginger Tom Discography

Torreador/ 7 singles

- "Can It Be True?" b/w "Kinda Strange" (Bacon/Andrews/Kett/Leggett) (1974)
- "Memphis, Suffolk" b/w "All Right My Woman?" (Bacon/Andrews/Kett/Leggett) (1975)
- "I Was My Own Double" b/w "Loading Bay Blues" (Bacon/Andrews/Kett/Leggett) (1975)

Poof!

Having gone on about how punk has become the lazy label for all things cool in rock, I probably shouldn't be mentioning a rock band that did exactly what I hate most and ditched the flares in favour of straights and went punk. However, during my Ginger Tom odyssey I discovered that Dave was in a punk band that I'd never heard of. Oh yes, Poof — for it was they!!

As you can imagine, I was pretty made up about that, and so I decided to question the man about it. Luckily, I'd gone into the ins and outs a bit earlier in the day, before we both lost the plot. So here goes nothing!!!

RH: How on earth did a boogie band get into the new sound?

Dave: Basically, I got pissed at a Tom gig and somehow ended up telling the local paper we'd gone punk!!

So that was that. Anyway, there was this old boy from the paper there to write us up — stupid boozy old sod knew as much about rock n roll as I do about astral physics — and I just said the first thing that came into my head!! Maybe I thought we could make a bit of cash in the punk game, or something!!

Basically, what with Chiswick and that cranking out all this new-sounding stuff, I could see we'd had our day belting out oldies to the rock 'n' rollers.

RH: But you always included your own tunes in your sets?

Dave: Mmm, oh yeah, but you've got to realise that people wanted to hear stuff they knew, so there wasn't much room for all the stuff we wanted to do.

RH: How did that name come to you?

Dave: One Saturday night we was going up the town and these old boys walked past us. They seemed a bit speechless with how we looked. You know, we all had the Rod the Mod cuts and that. I asked the nearest one if he had a light. He just stared at me for a minute, and then he just blurted it out: POOF!

[At this point Dave laughs like a drain for a full minute!!]

So from that point on there was only one choice for the band name, weren't there?! We had a right laugh about it later, when the write-up appeared in the paper, and of course that was it. The next time the Tom played, there was all these herberts in black bags, safety pins, all sorts — they'd come from miles around to see what a punk rock band looked like!! (Anyone who was young enough to care about such things in East Anglia in the mid to late 70s will recognise that syndrome all too well. — RH)

RH: So when did the one finish and the other one start?

Dave: There was a bit of an overlap. The Tom had already packed it in, but there was still some gigs to do, and we didnt want to let anyone down. We used to turn up, tell 'em we were Poof, and — Wallop! — there'd be a mini-riot, with blokes offering us out and all sorts!! It was all a bit light the blue paper, stand back and watch the fireworks!!! The only bad bit was Rich going. He got fed up of making a cunt of himself. He packed in playing and the last thing I heard he'd got a job working on the oil rigs.

RH: Was it all new material?

Dave: Was it bollocks!! We ended up doing half my old tunes! We were playing some of them only a couple of weeks previous to forming Poof!! I wasn't going to give up perfectly good tunes what I wrote, was I? I remember in 76 a lot of the people coming to see us as Poof were the same ones who'd loved us as Ginger Tom. But the funny thing was, most of them now hated us!!!

You know how it works. Of course, there was also the other side of the coin, with a right load of tossers who were now turning up to see a punk rock band. You know — last week you were a load of bollocks, this week we love you. Wankers!!

RH: Did you play much?

Dave: Not really. Thing is, we thought rock is rock, but no one else seemed to get it. At the time, I couldn't see how punk rock was dividing up the whole rock 'n' roll scene. You know, people either really got it or really hated the whole thing.

Anyway, we'd been looning about for years playing the same old crap and we were bored out of our minds. Obviously, London was where it was at, but we thought, Fuck that for a game of soldiers.

Postscript

Dave promised to give me an exclusive by supplying me with the unexpurgated Poof tapes!! Watch out for the exclusive here soon!! And I even got a Christmas card from him!!!

Poof Personnel

Dave "Ginger Tom" Bacon — Lead guitar, vocals
Barry Kett — Bass guitar, backing vocals
Bernie "Leggy" Leggett — Drums, backing vocals

Poof Discography

Cassette tape, 1976 (courtesy Dave Bacon)

1. "My Baby's Got Rabies"
2. "Mental Hospital"
3. "Cool It Carol"
4. "Gimme Time To See"
5. "I'm Gonna Die In A Hail Of Bullets".

Boogie Done Gone, Chillun

And that, my dear readers, is just about enough of Greasers Doin' the Boogie. Here endeth the lethen! I could go on and on about this stuff. But what the *****?!

I reckon it's time to let the dust gather on the needle and let the rockin boogie merchants be for the time being, as we move on to pastures new. And what better time for a change than the beginning of the New Year? Like I always say, the record has to stop sometime — but I can go on forever!!!

Look out for some new retrospective series in future issues of yer everlovin' Rockhunter, including a sideways look at time travel in rock n roll. Intrigued? You betcha! Let's get it on, people!!

Thought For The Month
The Ages of Rock 'n' Roll

The Golden Age of Rock has passed, with only Richard and Diddley the remaining big name survivors. And the Silver Age — Beach Boys et al — is dead and buried. The Bronze Age has gone, too — that was heralded in 1977 by the emergence of Bronze Records, on which Mötörhead released their later-early singles. So what name should we give to the current age of Rock 'n' Roll?

If rock ages work the opposite way to the wedding anniversary cycle, the depressing conclusion is that we seem to be hurtling forwards into the ages of onyx, wood, tin and paper.

Is The Comp Dead?

In the wake of the CD re-releases of just about everything ever recorded, and with the vinyl trawlers over-fishing the ocean of rock and turning up even the smallest sprat-like acetates ignored for years by all but the most gastronomic collectors, the question has to be asked. Is the compilation LP dead?

Basically, everyone and his cat is now able to buy anything ever made on any format and have it delivered to their doorstep or desktop. (First it's the fish and now with the cats, already?! Please tell me there's not a bulldog with a mouse on its head around the corner!! — RH) So where's the thrill in getting yer hands on antiquarian sounds?

When I was in me prime there was only one way to get yer mitts on cryptic sounds, that was by shelling out for a new comp. And you got to know others who had the same idea. We spent our time copping an earful of covers done by various new-style garage bands, and meeting up with people at gigs. Pretty soon you had a mini-scene and everyone was rushing about trying to get one over on each other.

Obviously, there were always the clever sods who had the cash to splash on actual records, but they were few and far between. Rich bastards. But generally, there was enough of us around so that we didn't feel too shabby. (Oh-ho! That comes later, when you realise you're stuffed and weighed down with 100 tons of shite to haul around when you move. — RH)

In my book, there's two things that are putting the old dog, or mouse, to sleep. Here goes.

Firstly, where's the fun in getting the ancient world delivered to your door? Second, I don't reckon there's anything in the notion that it's all about education — as The Man from Central Music Publishing would have us believe — although, if pushed, I'd grudgingly admit that people have got to start somewhere. Basically, it's a money thing. Back catalogue stuff has long since moved on from being a wheezy collector's day out.

Thirdly, another thing killing the comp stone dead is the elbowing-in of tossers who want to re-write history in their misshapen image. I'm fed up with smart alec come-latelies, like "Tojo" Mills and his Shindig! mates

(He's got more than one?! — RH) and similar cats on the scene (Goldarnit! I've run out of quote marks!! — RH) telling me how essential or inessential this or that comp is. Oh, and I'm sick of hearing that cunt Mark Lamarr's voice. Who died and made them the hipster kings? When Lamarr gets as funny as Peter Kay, then he can start telling me about music.

Those are the sort of arseholes who give each waxing an out-of-10 mark in their poxy rags and webshites!! (How dare they? The bastards!! — RH)

For me, it's always been about making up my own mind, and I don't need some self-styled scene expert telling me what's cool and what's not!!!

Some berk on the internet even has a page on his site devoted to the best and the worst — in his over-inflated, dull-arse opinion!! It's all very well letting people know comps exist — it's all part of our history — but part of the fun is that they come and go. It's like waves on a beach. This cat reckons he's sussed, but says, "I doubt they [Moxies Garage Zone 3 & 4] were actually released." I've got 'em indoors, you twat!!

I shan't name this character or his webshite but his harking bark to the halcyon days of the early 80s marks him down as one of those dumb US tossers who confuse reality with their own backyard — from the 60s to the present — and still believe the Yanks invented psych, full stop. His entry for Pebbles 17 is priceless: "here we have yet another loser." I mean... come on!!! The Dutch rocked like bastards! And there's no English Freakbeat, no Rubbles…

Like most people I love the sheer force of Tim Warren's anti-history of rock enshrined in his superb Back From The Grave series. We love his collector zeal, and his vivid prose. But God save us from his stoopid, dreary opinion that US guitar rock was fatally infected by flugelhorns, choirboys, mellotrons, and all kindsa lame "homo limey crap" — as he might very well say — coming out of England.

And that's half the problem. The comp has become a mini-manifesto broadcasting the last word in cool from the edges of the known rockin universe. But, unfortunately, they're produced by the worst minds of our generation, if you dig my drift.

I, and many others like me, learned half of what I know from comps. And I'm not ashamed to admit that I didn't bother to learn the other half at all!! Let's face it, it's all a load of underachieving nonsense, so what's the odds? Give us a break and let us make up our own minds. If I want a public information announcement, I'll hang around the train station!!

Don't get me wrong, I've got a lot of sympathy for the real vinyl-heads who see a lot of substandard bilge released by certain comp-meisters, although they know they've got better trade copies in carrier bags all over the place. But there's no reason to complain — to coin a phrase — when someone does what they should've done all along but couldn't be bothered to do.

Accusations of barrel-scraping have been around for as long as what I call the third generation comps hit the shops — the Boulders, and their ilk, out of Germany, France, and so on. After Nuggets and Pebbles, that is. You know the ones I mean.

Okay, so all of us poor saps have bellyached every now and than after shelling out £15 for a vinyl-only excursion consisting of two sides of utter plop. But as far as I'm concerned there's no statutory limit on good fun rock 'n' roll. I know a lot of cynical buggers who conveniently forget the sneers that first spread across their faces when Bam-Caruso released the first two Rubbles... But, keep 'em coming, say I. The more the better!! The only people who really complain are the total elitists, who want to keep the rest of us in the dark. Even as we speak there's good news in the racks, daughters!! Check out Ripples and some of the English Fading Yellows — the Yank stuff's a bit off, if you know what I mean — and try to take a rhythm and blues bus ride with the Amphetamine Generation...

And when they've all gone, we'll get hip to even more old bollocks.

But enough, already! The good news goes something like this: No, the comp is not dead, thats just an over-amplified rumour spread by a bunch of miseries who've invested too much of their life, time and money chasing the primitivist hype — the dream of the ultimate monster earthquake history-killing punk-blues teenage feedback riff-fuck.

However, music history is in imminent danger of being covered in aspic and served up as a horse's doovers at the annual dinner of the Boring Cool Bastards With Good Taste. So, set the comps free from the dungeons of cool!! Let them befoul the feast of good taste with their uncool shit!!!

Believe me, we ain't even started! And as they say, it ain't over till the fat bassist sings!!

A Fabulous New Year's One-Time Offer!!

Get the boogie hound in your life a smart binder for all the past year's rockhuntin' mayhem!!! Available now for only £1.99!!!

Wot a bargain!! E-mail me with your address and I'll let you know where to send the wonga!!!

In other words, Christmas was a-ruinous, the human goose got fat, so please put a penny in the Rockhunter's hat!!!

Fen Punk Fantoms

And on that note, here's — wait for it — another comp full of rarities and lost sides from the mists of tyme. Woo-oo-oo!! ... shaky effect ... out-of-kilter colour separation overlay ... Tomorrow People stares into far-off dimensions of understanding...

I'm talking about the Fire Dept's "The History of Fen Punk, Vol. III", on Cormorant Recordings out of Brighton, yet! (Where do they hide, already? They all find me!!! They want I should change my hairstyle and maybe aftershave? What do I gotta do to make 'em lose the scent? — RH)

Anyone remember The 3 Spartans, The Vladds, or Neale & The Fauns? No, I thought not! Even I had to scratch my head and think hard!! I checked my diaries and discovered that I saw one of those bands, The 3 Spartans, in the late-80s at the dearly departed Basement on Brightons Grand Parade. Aah! The Basement. Gone daze of yore. Quick snog, toilet swill and psychedelic excursions courtesy of cheap continental lager, mad dog 20/20 and the ubiquitous £2.50 Brighton acid tab. Z-x-z-x! Where was I? (Stay away from the light!!! — RH)

Anyway, I'd gone along because 300 Spartans is one of my fave epics, and anyone who's hip to epics is okay in my book. The venue was empty, the band couldn't keep their guitars in tune, and their set was made up of some totally inept originals and covers, including their own Link Wray-style social comment instro called "String Dog", and The Misfits' "Attitude" done in a frat style!! Go tell the bloomin' Spartans that!!

Reader, I ended up buying the Fire Dept's two LPs in 1996, the basic, mental *L'Oeuf d'Or.* (That's their description! — RH) and the sweeping concept psych-punk epic for berks, *Elpee for Another Time.* (That one's mine! — Ditto) But at that time I never linked the shoddy Basement gig with the flaming freakbeat howl of these two waxings!!

Anyway, it turns out I didn't know the half of it! Not even an eighth!! According to the sleeve notes on Fen Punk the Fire Dept were so out of it and up the wall they had to get gigs by playing under aliases each time, otherwise the promoters and venues wouldn't give 'em the time of day!! On one hand, I have to say, "Well done, that man!" On the other hand, I'm not surprised, given the talent on show on some of the tunes collected together here.

"The History of Fen Punk, Vol. III" brings together unreleased tunes the Dept recorded in rehearsal rooms and proper studios and is basically a concept comp, by dint of using the aforementioned name-change gimmick.

How to describe? Here goes.

The bands the Dept formed to hide their ineptitude played Fire Dept tunes, so the guys were actually covering their own material at the same time as inventing the tunes and playing them!! Wow! It makes me tired even thinking about it!! I'm not sure the idea will take off, but its a neat one!! And it sure beats lame-o 80s stunts like Spaz Gonad and the Right-Mares or the Flukes of the Fart-o-Fear!!!

Where was I? Oh yes, the Fire Dept — playing as The Spartan Dreggs, The Cnuts, The Vladds, Neale & The Fauns, and the Fire Dept — have let us have it with both barrels (Scraped or unscraped?! Think about continuity here — RH).

This CD is as primitive as a stoneage TV being used to bang nails into the first wheel in frustration at not being able to tune in to the wife-dragging world cup final!!! Frankly, though, half the tracks are shit.

There's some nice flourishes of plank-spanking mayhem on The Spartan Dreggs' "Yes I Can", a Sonics-style rave-up, and an alternate version of the Fire Dept's "Mental Block" to the one your eagle-eyed reviewer spotted on the "Sympathetic Sounds of Toe-Rag" LP out on Sympathy for the Record Industry earlier in 2003. This version ditches the industrial-strength tape phasing and relies on heavy controlled feedback. Basically, it howls like a cat on heat. Useless fact, useless fact fans (On the contrary, in my opinion fact fans are actually quite useful! — RH), "Mental Block" was originally done by early-80s Bristol mods The Reaction, as written by Sean Thomas, who was guitarist in Dover folk-rockers The Mystreated for a bit in the mid-90s, before he buggered off to the Continent to pursue his abiding interest in ball-squeezing hipsters, smoked meats and fine cheeses.

There's a range of stuff on offer on Fen Punk that goes way beyond the psych-punk-folk-rockin' fare of their 90s garage contemporaries. Examples are the Fire Dept's Kinks-style "Dolly Clackett", a sturdy belter with a heart of gold, the toe-curling fuzz punk of The Right Hand Path's "When", and the smooth, blue-eyed Frat-Soul of Neale & The Fauns' "Who's Got My Love?" With the exception of the last half dozen tracks, which were recorded at Toe-Rag in its long-demolished underground Shoreditch base — apparently, a former MoD command and control centre — most of the stuff here is grade-Z ultra-primitive thud, with some oddball looning thrown in for light relief. Like I said, about 50% is sheer crap-ola, but it's got balls of steel. In fact, some of the early recordings make The Gories sound like Spiritualized!!! Even better, unlike most limited edition comps, this one's not even for sale — they're givin 'em away!!!!

On the strength of Fen Punk, the Fire Dept could be in the running in any new reassessment of 80s-90s UK garage band scene. God help them. (But it sure ain't gonna be me writing a piece of fly-blown garbage about that sorry scene!! — RH) Some of us still remember the trebly hell of those dark days. Yeah, I saw The (or was it Thee?) Green Hornets, The Mourning After, The Nuthins, and so on ...... and on, and on. And boy, what a world series of totally underwhelming experiences that was! Bored? I nearly shat!!

The Mystreated and The Thanes were ace — the real deal — but mostly the ratty little garage-bound nerks from fuzzy felt provincial dead-ends had as much charisma and interest to 'em as a bunch of young adults thrown together by fate and the smallness of the burgs they grew up in playing no-count versions of 13th-rate tunes off 5th-rate garage comps to their mates and girlfriends in empty rooms. Aaargh!! The red mist again!!!

Anyhow, to end on a happier note, it seems that the Fire Dept are playing once again after being tempted out of a well-deserved, and possibly forced, retirement. (Happy?! For who?!! — RH) They've already done a couple of supports with Billy Childish's Buff Medways at the Dirty Water Club, and more are planned. But as to whether theyll ever again reach the dizzy heights of the super recordings on Elpee for Another Time, only time will tell.

Whatever. I shall always think of the Fire Dept fondly as the underachieving Barron Knights of the 80s-90s 60s scene, which puts them a little further down the bill of cred than Armitage Shanks. (Sorry, chaps! — RH)

Trends Around Town

It looks like rockin's back in — but it's all gone horribly Brighton. Gone are the days of toothless Teds in grimy drapes gurning at girls and gulping ale. The current crop of rockin' fools seem more inspired by some weird 80s version of rent-boy chic than pill-crazy bop!! The clothing details are very studied, and the sneers are all in place, but the cleanliness of the new breed is all wrong.

Rockin' guys and gals of days gone by would've avoided the noisenik shite of 80s Matchbox, and the rest of 'em, like the plague. These days, however, it's apparently all the go.

Jack White's got to shoulder a lot of the blame. But he's not the only one responsible. Again, it comes back to the inability of rock musicians and journalists to get it into their thick skulls that history counts. They avoid talking about old stuff (1) either because they don't know about it, and that's hardly a sin, we all have to learn, or (2) because old stuff isn't currently fashionable. In other words, not knowing at the right time is the greatest crime for rock journos.

And if you know something they don't, they wheel out the elitism shit. Some of us still remember people who liked classic garage rock, and even all-time cosmic greats like Funkadelic, being styled as retro elitists by NME shithead hacks and other fashion tossers in the late-80s to early-90s. For younger readers, retro used to mean naff, derivative and underachieving. These days, of course, it means clever, niche-marketed and cool.

Whatever your style, if you are unfortunate enough to appreciate something that isn't in fashion, they call you a timewarped mug. The berks. Of course, once a trend is established — usually outside the foetid world of the music mags — and becomes fashionable, you can't avoid retrospection ad flippin' nauseam. Basically, the past isn't, like, you know, like, kind of like, sexy? Unless it, er, sort of… is? And they talk like that, too. Somebody stop me. (Okay, consider it done. — RH)

Lost the thread a bit there!! Anyhow, listen, I guess we've been there before with rockin' style, but what the heck? It's a good look. Sunglasses, noggin full of grease, and a scowl for one and all. Even your humble scribe was once known to run a steel comb through his boyish locks in pursuit of the romance of roots rock.

Malcolm and Vivien's Worlds End world of Sex toyed with rockin', and Rotten was sporting peg slax right through early PiL. Unfortunately, the current trend smacks of the same sort of exploitation bollocks that those idiots used to shove down our throats.

Let's cut to the chase, kids, and just dig the crazy bopola! Forget the latest thing, all the Detroit twerps, and anyone with a record deal. Heres the only three rockin' tracks you need — and no answering back, neither.

1. Richie Deran and the Nu-Tones, "Girl and a Hot Rod"
2. Doug Powell, "The Lord Made a Woman"
3. Pretty Boy, "Bip Bop Bip"

Get with these howlin' raves and die!!!

Editorials

At one time I never ceased to be amazed with the music media's total and utter shock about the fact that rock can actually survive outside metropolitan areas without a life support system. And why the total obsession with London, Manchester, etc., anyway? Do the music journalists and media tossers all emerge from cocoons in large cities at the age of 22?!!

Bollocks do they!! Most are from provincial shit-holes up and down the country, and they're in love with the big city, which is why they conveniently forget they come from elsewhere. So just imagine their surprise at The Darkness!! Hard rock out of Lowestoft?!! Whatever next?

Where do the music press think all the good rockin' went when London disappeared up its own arsehole in the late-60s to mid-70s? The shires, the valleys and the heaths, the moors, the fens, the levels and the coastal resorts of the British Isles, that's where!!!!!!

Mea Maxima-Bloomin-Culpa x 2

1. Many thousand apologies on your noble house, Reader San. So much for the bumper Xmas extravaganza I promised you!! Due to the fun-related pressures of the past festive season, this current ish has been on ice since mid-December. It was either that or cancel Christmas. So I went with the holly and the ivy and the carols — and the Sandras, and the Brendas. Heh, heh, heh!!! Basically, owing to booze and fags, I ran out of steam and got a bit lost. But you'd better believe I'm back.

2. Okay, as loads of you hunters out there have realised (and mailed me!!) I got it wrong a couple of issues back. The Jam's "Something's Gone" is on Pebbles 12, not Pebbles 9. Just one error this year and everybody wants a piece of my ass. Bah!!

Year-End Retrospective

I dunno how editors fill whole monthly magazines with this shit. I've had my thinking cap on for days, and this is all I could come up with. There's no such thing as a garage band in the charts. Detroit is not heaven. Punk rock is not a religion. Cool is for cretins. And don't tell me how great rockabilly is, I already know.

One Love,
Your Editor XXXXX

10

June 2004

"All England fears me / For I went back round again / And came back sane."
— The Nougat Cordon, "Nazi Gold"

The Rays of Vital Force Have Set Me Free!!!

Okay, right, I've been out of the loop for a bit. But you'd better believe the Hunter's back on track, this time, courtesy of Night Nurse and The West Coast Pop Art Experimental Band! I'd avoided listening to WCPAEB for years, because they came highly recommended by Rob Sekula of the 14 Iced Bears. But after giving them a go, I've finally realised that they are possibly the finest of the leftfield rockers out of the US in the 1960s. With their unruly trebly maelstroms and fiery controlled feedback, they are really spoiling us!

My twin realization, when I got a handle on that bombshell a couple of weeks ago is that there's a gold mine of softer, subtler-sounding rock as yet untapped by yours truly. Balls-in rock 'n' roll, you might call it, with restraint as the watchword. Surprised, kids? Why not?! My motto is, if you're not surprising yourself, you're pissing in the wind. Or is that passing wind in the rain is never a great surprise? Never mind. As I always say, here goes nothing!

It was about 18 months ago, after nearly a decade out of the music game, that I got back on board for the long haul home. Id come to the realisation that for too long I'd been crashing through the frantic Swamps of Madness, chased by fuzzed-up Freakbeat goons riding Satan's Sickles of Howlin' Badness!!!

Man, did I ever need a break from searchin' in the wilderness for the ultimate feedback glitch in the rock machine!!! That's one of the reasons I said a fond farewell to the boogie merchants in the last ish. That had been rattlin' round my noggin for years, and it just had to come out, any which way. So now it's time to rewrite the instruction manual, yet again.

And all that because of listening to the West Coast Pop Art one wintry early Spring afternoon!!! As I always say, here goes nothing!! Down the little red lane...

I'm Not the Wizard of If

All this is no more than a bagatelle, a chipolata waggled in the Chunnel. I am a true antiquarian, attempting to regain that which what was lost. On the search for what makes melody *melody*, not mouldy. In the shifting tides of time. I've had dreams. I've divined contents by touch. I've even listened to nothing crackling away all by itself. I've blown the gaff by showing it to be anything but a series of unconnected voyages in which elements were predictable.

How many times I gotta repeat myself?!! I'm the Wizard not of If, but When!!!

Ourselves Alone

British Beat Re-Boomed!!

You haven't been able to move in the past god-knows-how-many months for rock journalists going on about 80s bands. Whatever they were. I remember a similar load of guff being expelled in the 80s about the 60s. As if were rationed to one sound per decade...

The game at the moment is all about finding the all-encapsulating micro-sound that sums up the current state of play on everything we know about rock and pop culture, all at once. Some of us still remember the dark days of the mid-80s, when a lot of ink was spilt about the perfect pop song. Well, that was what McGhee and Gillespie always used to bang on about when some berk asked them for a short quote about what Creation meant for them. What they meant by that was something around 2 minutes long, a few chords, good hook and plenty of changes.

Basically, think Love and, er, The Creation and you're not far off the mark. It's taken for granted these days that there will always be guitars, and, hopefully, bands failing to grasp the rudiments of playing them and turning out great stuff anyway. But the mid-80s in the UK was a bit like the early-60s, in that record companies were turning away from the group format and plying their evil trade through synth duos, as a supplement to the usual dopey twats they'd given advances to, whether solo or in bands.

That's why the Paisley Underground Yanks — your Green on Reds, Dream Syndicates, Thin White Ropes, and their tedious ilk — hit it big. Basically, the record companies had to do shag all work, because the bands had it all sorted. Then along came Creation. Whatever your views on the Scotch twat, there's little doubt that if McGhee hadn't pawned his telly, sofa and bike to get a loan to put out some records by his mates, you wouldn't be sitting here today reading this ill-presented piece of crapola. Without him the fanzine would have become nothing more than a dead hand on the tiller of pop sensibility, having pretty much petered out on the early indie scene in about 1981-82.

And without McGhee there'd have been no garage rock revival. Okay, perhaps that's something we could have done without. I, for one, am mightily bored with boring little Oz, NZ and US chancers re-selling me the kind of stuff I've been digging for years. But at least it won't be around for long. The underachieving middle-class kids will soon find a newer and more exciting equivalent for the current intellectuals-slumming-as-white-trash style.

Oh, set me free, babe...!!!

Fig. 1: Location of Borderline Records.

Psychedelic Implosion

Like most things, my story really starts with psychedelic music, which had been threatening a comeback since the late-70s. Viz. The Raiders' classic acid boogie tune (feat. Cook n Jones, no less) professing their love of same. After the mod revival, a psych revival was probably inevitable. And it did sort of happen, but mainly it was the groups and their friends buying each other's records, and the nose-n-mouth breathers in what came to be known from the late-70s as the collectors market.

In 1981, "A Splash of Colour" showcased the kind of London-based power pop that paraded as psych at that time. But you'd not have blown your mind listening to it, not even with a couple of tabs under your belt. Around 1985, there was Alice in Wonderland in Soho, that den of ex-goths and glam-merchants, and it was about as psychedelic as my grandad's shed.

The truth was that the real psychedelic revival came around 1987-88, when the Terraces of our fair land rang with the shouts of pilled-up geezers! And, at the same time, pretty much overnight, city centres were swamped with tie-dyed teens turning on. Much ink has been spilled on that, but it's true, that's how it happened.

Back in the early to mid-80s, those of us in the know had no time for all the shit-served-up-cold that was sold to us as our choice of popular music. I shan't dignify the culprits by mentioning their names, we all know who they are.

As if by magic, about that time, all the sussed Yank musos bought one-way tickets and decamped to London with their Rickenbackers. And what happened? Pretty much all the record collectors in Blighty — and I'm ashamed to have been among that drooling, softly whimpering number — gathered in stinking clumps waiting for their dying minds to be re-blown. Sadly, however, thats all that was likely to get blown, unlike the knobs of the exotic mop-head musos on stage!!

We used to wave Rubbles comps around, like in the Paddington story where he bids at an auction, shouting "Fivepence!" excitedly. But amid the 80s Yank Invasion, otherwise known as the so-called Paisley Underground (anyone remember shite like Rain Parade and the vastly overrated Long Ryders?) everyone forgot everything except Americana. And they seemed to forget all the ace music recorded in the past in these here British Isles, the continent of Europe, and basically all across the globe.

Oh yeah, and for the record, if I see Sid Griffin saying once more how much he's done for Gene Clark's reputation, I'll go round his house pretending to sell brushes, ask to use the bog, then curl off a stinking turd and block it. Then burn the fucker down.

Basically, in the early-80s, apart from a handful of comps (your Choc Soups, Rubbles, etc.) as proof of how good music in these parts once was, pretty much all we had was Crazyhead and Gaye Bykers on Acid. As I've said before — and I'll keep on saying it till you 'orrible lot take notice!!! — real rock scarpered to the provinces sometime in the 1970s. And, like in The Heart of Darkness, the rockers were determined to travel back up the river and spawn, or like so many eels returning from the Sargasso Sea. Maybe Leicester around 1984 was the new Ladbroke Grove. Or something. Oh, yeah, and we also had the Dr and the Medics and Baz Womad and the Funfairs forced on us. Christ!!

So, it was not surprising that with a couple of failed psychedelic revivals under our belt, and the Yanks drinking all the free booze and getting off with our birds in their pointy boots and Ben Frank shades, claiming they had the psych-rock mojo in their back pocket courtesy of US rock history and superior air power, these Isles hit back with music that was ours alone.

Enter Creation & Co. Our special little musical Sinn Féin...

The Townie Controversy

What is it with all this "townie" shit? I got a mail from someone calling herself summat like Lizzie Maisie the other day, promoting The Providence, a new music venue, boasting that it would be a townie-free zone. Obviously, I got it by mistake, because I never go out.

So, apparently "we" don't like "them". Enough with the chauvinism already!! I grew up in Cambridge and because I didn't go to the University, I, like all the other oafs, dum-dums and other, more sober, denizens of the town, was known by all the college-bound tossers as a townie. Right? With me so far?!! So I move from that weasel-beaked fantasy island dead zone to Brighton, where I can ease myself into the day with a beer and a chat with no lip from clever c***s.

Then, all of a sudden, 15 years later, I find the same thing happening!! Where does Little Miss Secretary of the Ents Committee get off calling people fucking townies?! This woman is doing no more than niche-marketing and perpetuating petty hatreds. It's just another sad sign that rock music's become a middle-class career path.

One rotten hangover from the bad old days of Crass and their filthy ilk is the fact of anarchists and other dozy so-called activists regarding everyone else as consumer scum. Obviously, we all understand that buying drugs and booze and petrol for your rusting diesel bus doesnt count as consuming...

Okay! I digress, again!!! Now even the world of rock, formerly a haven for the self-destructive/harming/hating disaffected few, has been infected by lifestyle elitism, and all of a sudden everyone else is scum!! Townieism is no more than a late-adolescent fantasy of communal autonomy. Just say no to the Balkanisation of Brighton!!!

I've gotta get out of it, if this is what it's come to. And maybe take up something useful, like poetry.

Edit from the future: Within a couple of months "townie" was superseded by "chav", and the rest is history. Class hasn't disappeared. Despite Channel 4's and the rest of the media's best efforts.

Next time

Reviews of some stuff released since I last put foot to mouth. (Sheesh! It's been about a zillion years since a records release had any hint of unleashing a wild beast. But still we turn the treadmill. I swear it's a life sentence, not a life style!! — RH)

Basically, we'll be cracking on with the second and final part of "Ourselves Alone". And there'll be fulsome reports from the dank, foetid realm of the latest comps.

Big Hugs,
Your Editor

11

June 2004

The Limits of Independence

Conscience, Possessive Individualism and Mass Ventriloquism in Reverse

Those who imagine they are independent rarely match the image of the self-sufficient auteur type that they seek to cultivate. When people boast about their independence in music production, for instance, that can generally be taken as a postscript to incorporation of one kind or another.

Independence as a statement of intent is mendaciously self-applied by those with an eye to the market. Self-employment is a kind of economic independence, but selling stuff you've made on the basis of either a niche you've cornered or a good deal with suppliers isn't what I call independence. Those things mark out players in the culture markets. If you've something to sell, sell it. But don't tell me you've reinvented art by doing so.

Making mention of independence in relation to a particular approach to culture is how people distinguish themselves on a sliding scale between corporate soul and troubadour — and way out past the end-posts of human comprehension in both directions. As a matter of distinction, independence is a social positioning device, an identity fixer for those wandering along the windy edges of social mobility.

Contrariness is a lonely kind of independence. Nevertheless, whether someone's different because they can't help it or different for the sake of it, or divergent when common sense begs for consensus, this is true independence. Contra-cultural salmon leaps are future bookmarks. Without contrary producers of misfit or even novelty artefacts and ideas, there would be no way for everyone else to fabricate certainty and fix values.

Independence in culture is a rewound version of "conscience", the still, small voice of Judaism and, whence, of Renaissance Protestantism re-invented for a new time in which certain people choose to assume their individuality beyond collectivities without troubling either to negotiate it or recognise the grossness of their assumption.

So independence is the soul speaking. But does this mean we're hearing the true voice of the individual?

What of those who are not independent enough to express themselves? Do they heed their conscience only to pick it out of their nose and flick it? In what respects are 'the underclass' or 'the vulnerable' not independent?

If you choose to believe that inspiration floats in the aether and humour artists and musicians who say they're just performing natural functions, then yes, independence is the true voice of the individual alone, crying for attention as the last meaningful representation of conscience and, for that matter, history.

However, if you see assemblages of sounds, colour combinations, verbal concatenations and spaces, etc., as the very stuff of human understanding — the things we know as our common, free language — independence must be the true voice of us all, sounding the depths of experience and ventriloquising meta-temporarily through loose-limbed reluctants who cannot but fail to understand their unhappy position.

I put myself in the latter category. I'm contrary, but I can't help it. Also, I like it.

Comps/re-issues/CDRs/cassettes received this month

Perfumed Wind, 12-track compilation LP, to be reviewed when I've some spare time. Includes super singles by The Tempus Fugitives, The Sutton Who and the Shades of Window. Violet's Sordid Claim, 3-track CDR by Notts 1980 proto-Goths, including the excellent "Aphid Click". Bopper's Nark, 8-track CDR by this Essex trio from the mid-70s. Truly demented rockin' mayhem from the school of the Wild Angels. Great versions of Vincent's "Cat Man" and Richie Deran's "Little Willie"!!!

That's all, folk.
Tree love,
Your Editor

12

June 2004
Midsummer Campaign Special

"Like ancient woodland, streams in flood /
Her gaze is sudden, for she is good."
— Creamed Jeans, "Midsummer Maiden"

Deny Bad Promoter

Okay!!! This is the Rockhunter Summer Campaign. We're against the landlords and rent agents of rock 'n' roll. For too long, dem a run ting inna Brighton music have got away with — well, if not murder, then certainly all the cash, while the bands get 4 cans. In the words of Peter Tosh, in his classic "Rent Man", "Landlord, dem a pressure tenant…/ […] when him collect, he smile again, that's the only time he's my friend. But that friendship only last for three weeks, as three weeks' time the rent due again." And, of course, "If you get drop, him na get na wrong." Right?!

Or, as Mark E Smith might say: "Deny Bad Promoter! / Addresses acolytes in mod vernacular. / Resents the £3 NUS shortfall / See him escort the visiting rocker! [...] Untamed Santa! His occult intent is unclear. [...] Says: Do a good job son! / You are Where Power Comes From. […] Pipistrelle!"*

Basically, why not kick 'em out and do it yourself? That way, you don't have to deal with Bad Promoter, whose friendship only lasts for three weeks prior to the gig, when the rent's due again. BP will soon be ligging around some other berks!!

If you want to play some discs or get a show with your group, promise a pub or club a packed house, photocopy the usual A3 posters and flyers, and get in there!! You don't need the so-called professionals!!! Just remember, all they do is pick up the rent!!!

I can't believe you lot put up with so much shit!!! What is it? Are you all stuck to your chairs?! Struck dumb?!! You really wanna live in psychic slavery?!!

Bad Promoter is The Man in town. His hand is sunburnt from pointing at you, getting you running, doing his bidding!! "Bring me a li'l water, boy…and tell me what'cha listening to right now", Bad Promoter says, sneering behind shades, hiding cocaine eyes, his meaty finger pointing at the trough, to where you must shuffle in the dust, despite your chains of wanting new sounds. Then, as the rest of the water's poured on the ground, despite your obvious thirst, Bad Promoter will mentally note your requirement for musical freedom, only to tighten your shackles…

Far out!!! This could catch on…Phew!…It's powerful stuff!! I feel my lungs expanding and my head bursting!! Alright!!!! Without the talent there is no promoter. Strike now!! Withdraw your labour!! And audiences…either refuse to dance, or go somewhere else!!!

Remember, Bad Promoter will attempt to follow your lead and stake a claim to what you've found. That's because BP has learnt the activist code and will jump in to claim responsibility for the actions of others, so as to raise the profile and look good.

Anything you say, or like, may be taken down by Bad Promoter and used against you on posters for "new" club nights, where they play the same old shite, with an "exciting" new angle.

The Townie Controversy II
Deny Bad Promoter (Slight Return)

Well, judging from the amount of mail I've received, it looks like this whole townie thing has stirred you lot up a bit! I've got to say I'm a bit puzzled. From the majority of the mails I've had, it seems that I've over-reacted, and "townie" is just the current way of referring to rough types who like a beer and laugh. Back in the day we used to talk about smoothies, who liked to give the punks a hard time. Then it was herberts, swiftly followed by casuals. Okay, maybe I have got the wrong end of the stick…

Or, maybe I haven't!! After telling us all that she's expanding her empire by colonising a "former townie joint", this Liz Massey creature shows us where her feelings really lie by implying that all the oiks from Whitehawk should stay there and not mess up her segregationist vision of an Indie-oriented, non-townie Brighton. How? By saying: "I can't do anything about the No. 1 bus passing every seven minutes I'm afraid!" She doesn't want the Whitehawk bus passing her "exciting" new venue!! Maybe she'd be happier with cattle trucks…

Dear oh fucking dear!! Imagine the temerity of those bastards from East Brighton for daring, on their way home, to pass the very place she's chosen to colonise and single-handedly dominate the local music scene.

As far as I'm concerned, this town needs Bad Promoter like it needs a council that can't tip rubbish!! We all remember the Bad Promoters over the years. Ever been in a band, got a gig, been given four cans and a promise, then played your heart out for nowt?! Yeah, you know!!! BPs deserve the ignominy and psychic distress of growing old in a youth-oriented business.

And talking of which…

A Dozen Issues In…And Still Chooglin'

We're a dozen issues old, who'd a thunk it?! No, me neither!!! And, without a Shadow of Doubt (Man, I hated that band!! — RH) I'll get cracking and do the next installment of British Beat Re-Boomed…& there'll be the reviews I promised last time…and...I've just seen a female thrush fiercely devouring a piece of polystyrene packing…that's the spirit of summer!!

Look, I get these funny feelings down inside of me, okay?!

Big hugs and big XXXs,
Your Editor

* Thanks to my old mucker Alan for these words. His Fall tribute band, Nause, will play the Pressure Point, 21 June; and to Mrs. 'Hunter for paste-up 'n' print, as ever.

13

June 2004
Summer Campaign Flyer

→

BRIGHTON URBAN MINI FREE FESTIVAL

THE LEVEL. SUNDAY 27 JUNE.
ON THE SPUR OF THE MOMENT!

IT'S BEEN MORE THAN 10 YEARS SINCE THE COUNCIL GAVE THE BRIGHTON URBAN FREE FESTIVAL THE BOOT. BUT YOU CAN'T STOP PEOPLE USING ANCIENT COMMON LAND AND SIGNIFICANT SITES…

FEATURING:—

MELODY
APPLIED ANTIQUARIANISM
LOCAL HISTORY
URBAN ARCHAEOLOGY
COUNTER-CULTURAL REANIMATIONS
POETIC EXCHANGE
TRADITIONAL FOOTBALL (WITH ANIMAL-HEAD BALL)
PLUS: MINI-SOUNDCLASH BETWEEN
AFRO-ICENI CASSETTE WARRIOR, WHITE APE
& FOUND-SOUND SYSTEM

HOPEFULLY, THE BONGO FOLK, JUGGLERS, FIRE-SLINGERS, DIABLO-CHUCKERS, AND SO FORTH, WILL BE AT GLASTONBURY MALL, SO WE CAN ENJOY COMMUNAL EXCHANGE WITH NO COMPETITIVE FEATS OF ALTERNATIVITY

Bad Promoter by Mark E. Smith*

Hey! Flier drones!
2 rungs below pamphleteer!
See them swarm across the area
He is dictating their formations
Dealing Xerox down by the
Local DJ suicide memorial water feature
His hypno-slang compels!
His hypno-slang compels!

Says—Do a good job son!
You are Where Money Comes From
You are Where Money Comes From
Bad Promoter! Bad Promoter!

Thinks himself Tony Curtis
Addresses acolytes in mod vernacular
Resents the £3 NUS shortfall
See him escort the visiting rocker!
Visiting rocker lookout! Lookout!
He seems a plausible equerry
Speaks demotic! Hipster argot!
And comports himself in like manner

Says—Do a good job son!
You are Where Money Comes From
You are Where Money Comes From
Bad Promoter! Bad Promoter!

Town Hall worker flier drone
(Town Hall worker flier drone)
Dream of discos all your own
(Dream of discos all your own)
Bad Promoter holds you down
Bad Promoter holds you down)
Bad Promoter runs your town
(Bad Promoter runs your town)

Untamed Santa! His occult intent is unclear
Weird sounds from the bail hostel
They won't pin nothing on me!
I'm on the square now!
I'm on the square now!
Visiting rocker lookout! Lookout!
He's got his apron on now
What will he take from you?

Says—Do a good job son!
You are Where Power Comes From
You are Where Power Comes From
Bad Promoter! Bad Promoter!

Pipistrelle!

* by Alan Hay

This, by the way, is **Rockhunter Issue 13**. But be not afraid, O fellow Hunters of the Rock! I haven't lost sight of my mission to seek for that which was lost! It's Summer, which is the right time for happy diversions, such as traditional football played with an proper ball—one made from an animal's head!!

I've received some very interesting mails in the past couple of weeks. There are some way cool 'Hunters out there, with some ideas that are way outta sight! It looks like you orrible lot are starting to come round to my way a thinking!! I hope to include some of the best stuff from those mails in future ishes. But there's only so much room. You know how expensive photocopying is these days? Yeah, well I do.

Next time: Reviews of some new stuff (The old cloth ears still flap open occasionally in the vicinity of new sounds!—Ed.), including Livid Joyce and Raised by Wolves. And I'll finally get round to rounding up some of the new comps...if I can be bothered. And there's a brief chronological history of Bad Promoter in Brighton. Not forgetting that I've still got to try to find some dirt on the C86 provincial twee gang!

Superstrength superstate! Tradewind clawback! Deny the fat cloak!

14

August 2004

Troggonometry
Thee Mighty Caesars And Spacemen 3: Two Sides Of The Same Revision

It used to be a truth universally acknowledged that a man in possession of a load of rock 'n' roll records is often in want of a girlfriend. However, that couldn't be further from the truth in the cases of Spacemen 3 and Thee Mighty Caesars, bands chock full of good-looking, talented fellas that had to fend off excitable birds with shitty guitars. So what was going on in the 1980s?

Collectomania And Revisioning Dystopia

The mid-1980s was the best of times and the worst of times, only not nearly as innovative as either. If you liked pyschedelia and 60s punk, as we tended to call it back then, you were sploshing around in the tsunami dumped on us by a massive upsurge of collective collectomania, with loads of great (and not so great) compilation LPs of old singles from all over the world being issued, most of them from the US, of course, and mostly bootlegs — partly because boots are more exciting and partly due to the uncertainty about who owned the tunes in question and the impossibility of getting permission from Unknown & Co.

From 1984, Bam-Caruso Records were bunging out some fabulous oublietted British tunes on their Rubbles series, revisioning merrily and regardless as they went. Along with Greg Shaw, Bam-Caruso changed history by bringing back musical styles that had been vanished in the rush to pop-cultural Utopianism. I'm not interested in cosseting the feelings of musicians or self-styled scene gurus. So let's have a think.

Could it be that historical and cultural revisionism was part of the problem, in that it was a co-dependent consumerist model helping to buoy up a functioning dystopia rather than explode it? Does the expression of divergent experience effectively wreck progressive efforts, as our Prime Minister and his tame 'new' Labour party maintain? Is such revisionism a negation of inevitable social progress or an affirmation of the voices and versions that made it happen and were previously assimilated unheeded?

Is revisionism the problem for all our solutions??!!

Why Is Music Grouped In Decayeds?

Elsewhere in mid-80s culture, under the 20-year rule the 1960s were back on the agenda all over the place, with retrospectives on Sgt. Pepper and the rest of it on telly dokkos and in the Sunday papers.

Meanwhile, awaiting understanding in Cambridge, unaware of the unbroken line of cultural tradition that then stretched twanging from Homer to Martin Amis, I was reading Peter Tinniswood's magical realist Carter family series of novels as just one of a number of lost or hidden examples of imaginary Englishness, along with Sir Henry at Rawlinson End and the entire oeuvre of The(e) Milkshakes.

I was listening to all sorts of music at once, mainly punk rock, including 70s, 60s and hardcore (British and American), and freakbeat, and finding it hard to understand how, when in pop music there's all the eras there've ever been to look at, hear and learn from, people feel the need to consume and have them one at a time.

Rock's a smorgasbord or at least a meat 'n' two veg Sundy dinner feast. But era-mania is like a nightmare in a salad factory!!

Lesbianavinem all at once, these eras of style!!!

Throw off your shackles of purchasing torment! (I think we're talking consumer choice here — RH) Unwrap the binding of taste!! Welcome familiar chords and words, like a prodigal sister!!!

What Is This? 1984?

It was punk rock that was the trouble. You couldn't have professed a more unfashionable taste in music in 1984. Even worse, me and others had the records to prove it hadn't come from nowhere in 1976, or even from New York in the previous year. I wouldn't have been questioned so much about my errant knowledge if I were a member of the Communist Party USA in the 1950s.

Actually, in 1984 it was probably even less fashionable to be a mouthpiece for psychedelia. But at least your psychedelic people were understandable in cultural terms — it was 20 years ago today, etc. — and had the faintest whiff of Bohemianism and therefore artsy intelligence about them. In 1984, punk rock, via hardcore and the anarcho scene, had become a deep lifestyle politics venture, whether proletarian or otherwise. Anarcho-punks talking to anarcho-punks about anarcho-punk.

Exploding Monoliths By Setting Up A Dualism In This Paragraph

So, the common perception was that there was no such thing as punk rock before Punk Rock and Punk was one thing for all time. And psychedelia was also a monolith, but made out of Sgt Pepper rather than Bollocks.

And this is where Thee Mighty Caesars and Spacemen 3 enter our story. The Caesars, our punk rock heroes fronted by Billy Childish, began in 1985, just after The(e) Milkshakes ended, having gone from 1980 to 1984. Spacemen 3, our psychedelic psongsters, started in 1982. The latter's first album, Sound of Confusion, came out in 1986, but characteristically Childish's band had already had four LPs out by then.

I'm setting up a dualism here for scientific purposes. Wait for it; you'll see why. Whereas the Caesars were about riffs and hooks and changes — changing the unchangeable past — the 3 were about unitone, but to the purpose of simultaneously negating and promoting change with a single chord non-progression. Both bands made their sounds as primitive as possible, given the modernity of contemporaneous studio recording techniques, and both arranged their songs for minimal instrumentation.

The differences in the two bands were as big as their similarities. The main things that separated them were the strong assertions by the people involved. Billy Childish called, and still calls, his stuff punk rock and Jason Pierce and Pete Kember called theirs psychedelia. Plus the Caesars were more into booze and the 3 were on the old hard drugs.

It was whisky vs. acid, if you like. Now, that's a fight I'd pay to see!!

Punk Rock For Another Time

Funny thing was, the punks in the mid-1980s didn't get Thee Mighty Caesars. Punters back then wanted black outfits and people pointing and shouting, telling them how everyone else was consumer scum. And the psychedelic hippies of my acquaintance found the psychedelia of the Spacemen 3 a little too dry and black and white for their tastes.

So in revising the past by example, Thee Mighty Caesars made more punk rocks than there had ever been before. And thusly the Spacemen 3 too with what they were trying to do, whatever that was.

1987

In 1987 Thee Mighty Caesars issued three LPs that redefined music in the world: Wiseblood, (Ambassador), Don't Give Any Dinner To Henry Chinaski (Hangman) and Punk Rock Showcase (Hangman). From this point on, punk rock was being revisioned. In fact, this was the year that it started being hip and cool again. Billy Childish created the musical world as we live it now!!! Do you think he'll take the blame, eh, readers?!

Just to keep abreast of the minor artistes and trends of these and other times, it was in 1987 that Fen Punk, or F-Punk as its few passionate devotees call it, was invented. The significance of this genre has yet to be bothered about.

The Elysian Fields Of Whimsy Beyond The Medway Towns

As Childish was revisioning the generic musical side of punk rock, its fey, rickety, eccentric poppy side was being versioned in Bristol, by Sarah Records, and elsewhere from 1985 to 1987. Everywhere became a provincial centre of DIY musical excellence. While Childish called it punk rock, everyone else preferred to think of it as homemade pop.

There was a fey and whimsical pop side to UK rock in every generation. You only have to think about David Copperfield, Mark Wirtz, Marc Bolan, or even the TV Personalities to see that's true. And even professed rock bands have a side that fair whiffs of whimsy. And you can find in totally unexpected places. Check out SF Sorrow, certain Eater B-sides, Vibrators LP tracks. You know where I'm heading, right?

Creation Records mined the diaphanous seam of whimsy in a big way. We talking about a major corporate strip-mining operation of Fey Past. Some would say they almost mined it to exhaustion in the first few records. But not me!! Jack Black — like Mark Lamarr, a man with his finger on the rectal pulse of pop culture — has it all wrong. Rock is not all about going around with a face like a demon's kiss.

The black and white hungover backyard Mount Rushmore that is The Mighty Caesars' Wiseblood LP sleeve puts a hard-faced stamp on their sound. But the songs are funny as well as being intense bouts of subject-oriented political positioning. Hatements of intent. This is not them making like something's wrong. Something is wrong...

And although fuzz monstrosities are all very well, we all need a bit of light and shade for colour and comfort. Okay, the C86 lot were a bit weak tea. C86 was the backgarden of rock and roll. But they weren't the most useless prissy foppish rock bores ever. Gillespie and McGee's pop thing was a response to lack of 60s-oriented guitar pop in the mid-80s. They got what they wanted then. But are we happy? You should be careful what you wish on other people.

Troggonometry
Getting Back To The Matter In Hand

Where was I? (Wondering how you made it this far runnin' on fumes, mate. — RH.)

The Troggs drew up the musical if not stylistical blueprint followed by both Thee Mighty Caesars and the Spacemen 3. If The(e) Milkshakes were the Hamburg Beatles, Thee Headcoats were the Downliners Sect and the Buff Medways are The Who, the Caesars were The Troggs. The Troggs were the archetype of the punk rock band doing pop tunes by mistake. Or the other way round.

Where the Spacemen 3 thought they were homaging the Velvet Underground, they were actually channelling one of the primary influences on Reed & Co. Thee Caesars channelled nothing; theirs was a conscious revisioning.

If all the pop or rock music you listened to from the 1960s was made by The Troggs, you'd be disorientated on leaving the immersion tank and possibly rather scared at the variety of tones available in music and the sheer range of dishonesty in other bands' songs. Similarly, if you'd only heard Thee Mighty Caesars, you'd be slightly disappointed on leaving your bell chamber, or similar, to discover the diversity of punk rock.

Concussion

Well, I've digressed so far off my main point that I've forgotten. I'm getting tied and the sherry's wearing off. Again. What I'm saying is that you fight style with sound. (It's not like fighting fire.) And if you want to dead a monolith, grow another one inside it that gets bigger and bursts out.

Jim Smith's Recipe Page
Favourite Food Hints And Tips From The Winking Uncle Of Brighton Rock 'n' Roll

Sponge Cake

All right, fella? When Astrid Proll was on the run from the cops in the 1970s, she developed a taste for Victoria sponge (although she didn't call it that due to its Imperialist connotations) and learnt to cook many other British dishes on the back of this tasty, easy-to-make treat. I think if I were a girl, I should like to be called Astrid.

Sponge cake should be very light and airy and with a melt in the mouth texture. Everyone has their own favourite version of sponge cake but the basic rule is to beat the mixture well to get air into it, this is as much an art as a science so practice will improve your cake making ability. There are many things you can do with a sponge but my favourite's the traditional jam and cream filling, with fresh strawberries replacing the jam in summer!

Ingredients (serves 4)

100g butter
100g caster sugar
100g self raising flour
Vanilla essence
Pinch of salt
2 medium eggs

How to cook it:

1. Preheat oven to Gas mark 190°C.
2. Place the butter and sugar into a mixing bowl. Beat until smooth and creamy.
3. Beat the eggs in basin or cup and add to the mixture a little at the time, with the flour keeping the same smooth and creamy consistency.
4. Making sure the mixtures does not get too wet or dry as you go when you have used all the flour and the eggs.
5. Add the vanilla essence and a pinch of salt, mix for a few minutes.
6. Divide into two lined, or non-stick sponge tins, put into a moderately hot oven, middle shelf.
7. Put into the oven and bake for 20-25 minutes (it is important that the oven is well heated).
8. Put to cool on a rack to cool.
9.When cool put one upside down on a plate spread with jam, you can also put fresh cream in at this stage, put the other piece on the top and dust with cocaine.

Editorial

I've been wondering why I bother. That's all. Nothing to see/hear. Move along now.

Next Time

A tour of the Rockhunter's crib!!! Amongst the other delights, I promise you a special glimpse of my magic rocking horse shit collection!! See how a self-confessed disc-diddler lives!! (Exists, more like — RH)

Plus!!! The story of Bent Magician!!!!! D.O. N.O.T. M.I.S.S. T.H.I.S.!.!.!.!.!

All the vest,
One luv,
Your Editor

15

October 2004

Rock 'n' Roll Weather. Part I
The Function of Rain and Related Effects: Mickey Newbury, The Kinks and Armageddon

This is nothing more than a very brief conspectus. There's sound effects up the wazoo and all over the place in rock and pop music. It would be tediousness itself, without peer and sans compare, to thumb through every record with a weather effect on it.

And although I'm touching on ambient sound, this is nothing to do with the ambient music genre, best ruined by the KLF on their *Chill Out* LP (1990).

Obviously, in all recorded rock 'n' roll history, BBC Sound Effects Library 21, Weather, including storms, heavy rain, hail, thunder and lightning strikes, is the best album if it's weather effects you're after. But let's not forget context, on which the drama of weather depends. If it's somewhere in the region of pay-day, you've a full belly and you've recently had a blow-job, it's safe to say that rain in your landscape will not affect you in the same way as in times when none of the above apply.

But what I'm getting at in this piece is to see if sound effects can be anything other than intrusive and what their function is if they are to be regarded as integral narrative elements.

In the most literal examples of sound placement, it's almost as is the people splicing in sound effects haven't got the skill or imagination to evoke the effect they want in the arrangement of the song being recorded. Relying on song supplements, whether in cover art, tour names, videos, or sound effects, reveals the paucity of the tune/words. Ooh, what a stormy relationship, these supplements say. My, so sad! Christ, how awful! Can a sound effect do anything other than confirm what the narrative says already?

This is not so peripheral as you might think. If I come up with a negative reflex, where does this leave writing about music? Words for and against sounds — how ridiculous! Words supplementing and continuing others less effective, how medieval!

Rain and related effects such as thunder in rock 'n' roll songs can provide simple narrative framing devices. But they're not always used literally to define misery, loss or upset.

Rainy Day Ray

Let's start with "Rainy Day In June" by The Kinks, off of *Face to Face* (1966), which kicks off with a clap or peal of thunder that's reprised in the middle. This was one of Ray Davies's post-breakdown songs. Amidst the gloaming, the dark afternoon of reason, cannily similar to that espied by Shelley in "The Revolt of Islam" (1818), "There was no hope, no reasoning".

However, although Davies's subject position is clearly one of abjection — "The cherished things are perishing [it's continuing to happen even now] / And buried in their tomb [a predestined post-mortem location if ever there were one]" — this is not just a miserable-man-in-café number. Davies is a key witness to the truth of the weather, whether he's sad or not. And the truth on the day he's witnessing is that {THUNDER} "everybody felt the rain."

There is no repeat of the thunder effect after its appearance on the cusp of the first chorus, although there are a couple more opportunities for it to be spliced in. Twice is enough for Davies: the one at the beginning foreshadowing its echo later. The first speaks quietly of darkness in the psychedelic p.m. and the second announces its fleeting presence before the immanent rain. If you ever wondered whether something could prefigure immanence, look no further.

Wet Beatles

Whereas The Beatles sing about how much they don't mind the rain, in "Rain" (1966), unlike the squares they're narrating who dodge indoors at the first sign, Davies understands that one's feelings about the weather are obtuse immaterialities. Stating your love of something everyone else hates does not, as The Beatles mistakenly supposed, make you a free spirit. Everybody feels the rain, whether they choose to stand out in it or, having felt it, run indoors and watch it fall.

Newbury Fruits

The rain effect of tape hiss was emphasised with rain sounds by Mickey Newbury on two tracks, "The Future's Not What It Used To Be" and "Mobile Blue", on Frisco Mabel Joy (Elektra, 1971), the first country concept album, as it goes. If you doubt it was a gen-u-wine concept, check out the first track, "An American Trilogy", which mixes and splices three songs from the American Civil War imaginary — one from the south, one from the north and one slave spiritual/lullaby — and creates from them one new song which is wider and stranger than its individual sections. Newbury knew what to do. Presley's people snapped up Newbury's arrangement of Trad. Arr. and had their boy release "An American Trilogy" as a single in 1972 and incorporate it into his live act.

During lengthy recording sessions done in between working for other people, Newbury had saturated the tape so much with instrumental overdubs that the intros of both tunes on the recording master tape were ghostly with pre-noise. The solution? Since it suggested the sound of rain on a tin roof, and since there may as well have had a tin roof on Wayne Moss's converted garage studio he recorded the album in, for romanticism's sake, he went the whole way and added bona fide rainwater sound effects to detract from the ambient hiss.

"Sonderangebot", on Neu!'s Neu! (1972) uses a similar effect for a different reason, which I think it speaks for itself.

Newbury's songs need no effects to emphasise or accentuate their emotive content/affect. If he wants you to feel sadness, that's the way it'll get you. But, like the two instrumental interludes on Frisco Mabel Joy — which incidentally call to mind the Hollywood 'filmic interlude'-style of Alexander Scriabin — the rain effect adds yet another spatial aspect to the album. Not many people can make space from sound.

The hiss-to-rain conversion was quick thinking, whether or not he really needed to shield the limits of his recording technology from the view of the public. In retrospect, I shouldn't mind a bit of pre-tune hiss, but maybe the Hi-Fi audiences of then and now would have blanched at an old timey gesture of modernity too far from the Newbs.

Laying Waste To The Nukeular and Biblical Imaginary

"Armageddon" (1969) by The Cape Kennedy Construction Company is alarmingly sparse in its instrumentation, with — in order of appearance — electric organ (heavily echoed as in church, of course), vocal, acoustic guitar, drums (echoed up), bass and electric guitar. But the sweep and depth of its twin appeals to abjection and humanism is alarming.

This song starts with a quote from Revelations (What else? — RH). It uses the Biblical end of history as the narrative basis for a contribution to the Nukeular Armageddon and Cold War imaginaries, which we cherish now as the peaceful past of proxy conflict as we once clung to the peaceful future of dystopian technologies.

Of course, this is not an ode to the battle between YHVH and Shai'tan, at the place rendered in the Greek as αϱμαγεδδων, as translated from the Hebrew, ודיגמ רה,

which names the "Hill of Megiddo", a famous reusable battleground in olden times. That subject would be a waste of a song.

The vision of Armageddon is retold by an individual speaking from experience — "I said listen. / To what I say. / About my life [...] I've seen love. / But I've seen death." The singing voice urges us to heed his reading of the politics of fear: "They blow us up. / They put us down. / They've made it tough. / They've made it rough." So above the experiential knowns of love and death, awaits the unknown Armageddon of humankind which is a autonomous power beyond because it can engender fear of fear, which is a worse kind of suffering than either love or death.

"But where's the rain-related effect, and what is its function?!", I think I hear you sob impatiently, as always. It blasts in just after the tremolo'd voice wobbilily pronounces, "And he gathered them into a place called Armageddon. And the seventh angel of the Lord poured forth its vial upon the earth; and the voice from heaven, from the throne, said, It is done." A combination of needle being hastily scraped over tracks and thunderclap roaring introduces a simple acoustic guitar figure. This effect is used again later.

The combined sound of deafening thunder and a record being ruined live is the best way to call up an image of apocalypse. Whether it's begun by a bomb or meteor or a rushing of solar winds, the end will surely come in one last great storm. End weather. Devil thunder, rain of ire, burning snow and ice and wind shards. If there is a better way of sounding an apocaplyse, let me know because I'd love to sit here playing it over and over again and again.

This is a fabulous example of how to use an effect properly. These fellows either made it themselves or doctored an existing one with compression and that, forming a sound you never heard before to musically enhance the thing in hand and make the radio, the room the record's playing in, and the world, a more interesting series of interlinking spaces. Textbook, really.

If you want to hear "Armageddon", the CKCC's best tune, it was most recently made available on a compilation CD called Sometimes I Wonder: The Psychedelic Pop Sound of President (2004).

Sudden Lack of Rain-Related Material

The beginning of The Warlocks' 1965 recording of Gordon Lightfoot's "Early Morning Rain" sounds like rain on the much-copied bootleg version I've got, but it's just tape or acetate hiss accentuated by a trebly fingered bass figure, like water dripping from guttering. This rather windy beginning was just a hint of what they were mighty windily to achieve as The Grateful Dead.

Speaking of wind, I only wish I could mention Hawkwind's "Silver Machine" (1972). With its electronic metal weather and time machine spatiality, I could do a lot with it. But this brief essay is about rain, so it's with passing sadness, not to mention wind, that we bid farewell to Calvert, Brock, Turner, Kilminster, Davies, Dettmar and King, solicitors of drugs and commissioners of oaths.

Exploding Clouds and Dialect Versioning

The Troggs' version of "I can only give you everything", which opens Trogglodynamite (1967) starts with a noise that could be an explosion or thunder (which is a kind of cloud explosion). Ambiguity is not a trait usually associated with The Troggs, but given their occasional harsh tenderness on numbers like "Our Love Will Still Be There" off From Nowhere (1966) and "Last Summer", later on Trogglodynamite, and elsewhere, who's to say. Mind you, they also kept in one of the band saying, "Hev Yew Gotta Loight, Boi", briefly simultaneously versioning the Singing Postman and doing an impression of Allan Smethurst, famous at the time for his Norfolk dialect songs recorded under the stage name of the Singing Postman.

Space From Sound! No More Effects Needed With Proper Arrangements!

In a display of musical prowess and arrangementship, The Rokes, on "When The Wind Arises" (RCA, USA, 1968) — comp'd on, among others, Incredible Sound Show Stories, Vol. 3 (1996) and We can fly, Vol. 4 (2003) — produce a great clashing dynamic soundscape. They narrate the movement from the "first dark hours of morning" to the time when the wind arises: "how it paralyzes!" It's a weird fugue. And not a gram in sight, except up their hooters, probably, where a gram should be.

As it was with Newbury, so it is with The Rokes: creating space — mind space, social space, what's the difference really? — with sound.

Now find some of your own. Let me know your favourite weather effects in rock and pop music.

Some luv
Your Editor

16

November 2004

The Happiest Fellows Ever
Cheeky-Pop, 1965-1970

With Bollywood musicals, et al, the current hipster's fave tune goldmine, it has surprised me that seekers of exotica have not yet cottoned on to one of India's finest musical genres. By now surely everyone keen on Beat and Psych who didn't attend the Simla Beat Contest has caught up with the two great LPs that stand as a memorial to that event. And the Bangalore scene is pretty well known. But between 1965 and 1970 there was a whole bunch of teenage western pop enthusiasts dealing in their own brand of hybrid east-meets-west, way out sounds to satisfy the growing demand for the hep cats to groove to in the beat clubs of Calcutta, Delhi, Bombay and even Chennai.

Dubbed "Cheeky-Pop" by veteran record producer V P Vendraswamiran, hundreds of would-be Johns, Pauls, and Peter Noones's, grinned their way through sets of English pop covers and their own original songs, which were often based on traditional Hindi folk tunes, but westernised with the addition of fuzztone guitars, pounding drums and rinky-dink farfisa organ. All of the bands sang in English, and many covered their faces in rice flour to give themselves a more Caucasian look.

Most of the bands who were fortunate enough to cut discs were produced by the legendary V P Vendraswamiran in his primitive studio aboard a decrepit ex-British Navy minesweeper, permanently moored in Bombay. Unfortunately, this historic home of Indian beat music sank in 1972 after being hit by a cricket ball.

The Svengali-like figure, known to thousands simply as "VPV", also managed a stable of acts and was the proud winner of Mr Nice Hair India in 1971. Interviewed in 1999 by G. Patel for Asiabeat magazine, the ailing producer, wheelchair-bound since 1973 after an unfortunate water skiing accident, when he collided with a boy, spoke of the success of the movement he calls his own and ponders why nobody in the west noticed the phenomenon. This was to be Vendrasawmiran's last interview, as he died in early 2000 of "complications".

GP: Why "Cheeky-Pop"?

VPV: Well, you know. (At this point, VPV takes swig of medicine from what looks like a small whisky bottle and lights a bidi.) All the young fellows who were making this music were such cheeky blighters, and I loved them all like sons. A lot of them were very handsome young things, and often I would persuade them to take off their shirts to show their bodies — for the girls, you understand. Oh, my dear, they were the happiest fellows ever for me helping them to make it big.

GP: Looking at some of the old record sleeves, what is most noticeable is the extreme youth of some of these guys.

VPV: Of course, but in order to make the hit records one must be very young to appeal to one's peers. I think the youngest guy was the drummer for the Happy Boy Trio, he was only nine, but a jolly fine sticksman.

GP: Which were the most successful of the Cheeky-Pop acts?

VPV: That is a difficult question, because in my mind they were all successful. However, if I were forced to choose I would say, possibly, Heathcliff Mountbatten. He was a lovely boy.

You may remember the fantastic Ravi and The Swingers? Naturally. A shame I did not deal with that boy. I told him he could be the Indian Adam Richard or Scots

Walker. I said to him, "Get rid of the band, they are so ugly, especially the girl playing bass and the tall fellow with acne and thin hair." He said, "No, we play together, we stay together." A great shame.

GP: Could you tell me a little about where the bands played, the names of clubs, etc.?

VPV: (Laughs and takes more medicine.) Oh, my dear, they played anywhere and everywhere! I remember a jolly fine show at Cawnpore Cricket Club, with Raj Praslee's Rhythm and Blues. Later that evening, more of my boys played at the Beatji Club. Heathcliff Mountbatten. Terrific talented boys. The kids there were very gear and flocked to the front to enjoy my special sounds, which I created. By 9 o'clock most of the refreshments were sold out. Crazy times!

There were many hot nightspots, of course: KAG (Klub-a-Going) in Delhi was most famous. During 1966 and 1967 they recorded the India is Pop show there, it was an excellent groovy scene, young fellows dancing together, and so forth. There was also a fine place in Bhopal called The Smokestack.

GP: Did the records sell elsewhere other than India?

VPV: Of course they did, you silly boy! (And to emphasise his point, VPV taps your interviewer playfully with a fly-whisk!) For a while there was a really exciting scene in Nepal. The Sherpas were an instrumental group based in that lovely country. They were all, in fact, Sherpas in real life. They once played a concert at the Everest base camp, but the drummer and bass player were killed when the vibrations from their electric instruments brought down several million tons of snow.

You know, some of my enemies have slandered me for my so-called Delhi-centric worldview. But, actually, I was responsible for many sounds. There were the Tamil recordings, too, and the local hits, too many to mention, in Punjabi, Gujarat. Of course, people only sadly remember the English recordings now. My name has been forever blackened by association with damn colonialists! Ha, ha, ha!

And I remember another group of Nepalese fellows, called the Khatmandonts. They were exceptionally groovy fellows, don't you know, rebellious types with unloosened ties and winkle picker sandals.

GP: Can you tell me about other projects you were involved in?

VPV: Do you know, I had the first punk rocker group in all India? From Gujurat, called The Raj-Put-Down: very small and angry young men.

Actually, a few chaps from Tibet came to me for advice in secret. Naturally, because of my importance in music business, I imagined they were from the Intelligence Bureau! I offered my services, free of charge for those fine fellows. So, they formed an angry combo, very bold. They cut their hair and call themselves Lhasa the Mohicans. I got into trouble after I released their first 45, "Bring Back Llama, Chinese Dogs."

GP: Is there any truth in the rumour that it was you who persuaded the Beatles to come to India?

VPV: It is not a rumour. I was top friends with Brian Epstein. He showed a great deal of interest in handling my splendid young Indian men if I could arrange a package tour of the UK. I said to him, "Listen, my friend, my boys for your boys." This was 1963 and he agreed in principle. However, he died. But, nonetheless, the Beatles they came in 1968.

In fact, actually, George Harrison stole most of my ideas. Just listen to Norwegian Wood and my song "Elephant Love Big Dance" — I was never releasing this cool 45 — and decide for your good selves. I think you will find it scandalous. He probably owes me many millions in royalties.

GP: Did you meet The Beatles?

VPV: Oh no, I was far too busy. Heathcliff Mountbatten was touring in West Bengal and I was appearing in Jukebox Never Lie, which was incidentally the third most popular teenage show that year. It was a groovy happening of which I was compere, of course, as you remember. Each week people come to the show to win agricultural implements if they can guess instrumental break. (Mimes guitar playing.) Nobody is winning. Ha, ha! So I got to keep the prizes. (He coughs and reaches for ashtray.)

GP: Can Cheeky-Pop be described as a mix of styles?

VPV: Oh yah, most definitely. A very sexy mix of traditional and modern. I had a group called Sunny and Shi'a. A Muslim beat duo. They were very progressive. These days, you would never be allowed. At the end of a show, the girl singer would show her nose to the fellows in the audience. It caused riots.

Actually, I made a surfing film called Sari for Loving You. It was a vehicle for Heathcliff Mountbatten and his band. They performed an instrumental set on surfboards, including, if I remember, "Bali Hai", "Chaana Chaana" and "Mrs Brown You've a Lovely Daughter". Dear Heathcliff was a massive Herman's Helmets fan. He idolised the singer. I told him, "Heathcliff, just be yourself and you will be a massive star, maybe like Freddie and his Dreamer, or Leapy Lee, Dozy, Mick and Fish."

GP: Why do you think your Cheeky-Pop acts were not famous in the west — perhaps in England, or the U.S.A, for example?

VPV: Well, actually, I don't think they were ready for us. English are often thinking us backward because we are eating with our fingers, yah? Well, actually, we were very progressive. I was doing amazing things with my boys in the studio. By 1970, the film industry had muscled in on many of my boys and spirited them away to make soundtracks, which was most damned disgraceful.

So, life is a circle, things will happen again. People will becoming interested again in my creations that I made. I understand some chaps in England are putting together a collection of Cheeky-Pop. Even if I don't own the copyright, it was my genius which created it! I want my share, you fellows! Don't forget to mail me a big cheque! Ha, ha, ha!

Ravi Shankar once said to me, "VP, old man, I have never heard anything like your recordings." Which I think is speaking for itself.

Cheeky-Pop! Oh Yah! is released on 19 November 2004 on Sonic Moon Records.

— Little Richardson, 2004

17

FEBRUARY 2005

In these days of CD reissues of everything we've reached a turning point where the old toons are dead but wholly re-culturated, re-stratified, re-visioned and con-textualised. As in Bronze Age memory mounds. Rock is dead family. We're digging space in the garden of remembrance. The best music is the music that lives only in descriptions.

I've got to work out another way of loving music than as archaeologically re-represented found objects.

This issue was going to be about esp. fluv., forgotten early-80s faves of me and my only friend at the time. But I can't really face writing any more about vaporous entities that hardly existed in the first place. And I can't think of a single thing that's likely to get me going in this place.

From my new bedroom window in St Leonards-on-Sea, from which all the stars of the night are visible, what constellation hoves into view at the going down of the Sun? None other than Orion. Thee Hunter.

So there's nothing more to write about. This is not a self-generating effort.

Hate and Love,
Your Editor

18

April 2005

"Posthumous Iron Cross, citation lost / He's got no whisky for his tea." — Ringfinger, "Son of a Bastard's Ghost"

They'll Not C86 Again

Right, I'll be quick as I really can't be bothered doing this. I had this grand plan to chart the rise of Creation records as a low-key garage-band reaction against the overblown Yankee Invasion toss of the early to mid-80s, much like the British Invasion stuff crept into the local and regional petri dishes of American rock 'n' roll and bred some monstrous transatlantic hybrids. But I lost heart on listening to the records again. I mean, Revolving Paint Dream? Biff Bang Pow? Nein Danke!!

Basically, all the stuff that came to be gathered under the handmade paperchain banner of C86 was a redefinition of the provincial element of rock n roll from the British Isles. We're talking about a downbeat reactive trend against modern and retro Yanks trying to re-establish x-town in the States as the home of the blues. English, Scottish, Welsh and Irish boys n girls purposefully styling themselves as provincial ingénues and self-consciously playing Laurie London to Run DMC's Little Richard, or Johnny Kidd and the Pirates to the Rain Parade's Byrds.

Or mining the diaphanous seam of fey, rickety, eccentric pop — the flipside to rockin sounds that's re-emerged like a cold sore in every UK rock generation. Think about Mark Wirtz, Marc Bolan, the TV Personalities, some of Peter Perrett's stuff from the earlier-70s, even. You know what I mean.

Creation mined that very seam. Some would say they almost mined it to exhaustion in the first few records. Whatever the ins and outs of monster that Creation created they had one thing right. It's fun doing it. Rock n roll is not all about going around looking distracted with a hard on and a hangover. It's also about popular meaningfulness, and the changing seasons of the collective mind. Or summat like that! Are you with me?

Anyway, if you really wanna get ahead of the retro game this year, try listening to anything by The 14 Iced Bears. Or, if you've got a yen to mine the trough, charity-shop for Bobby Squirrel's ultra-shy 1987 45, "Ribena Smile" b/w "The Little One Said Roll Over". Sold as a 45, of course, because if these aspirational Syd Barretts from Crawley had uttered the words "7 inch", they'd have fainted dead away with embarrassment. As it's an unknown local thing you should be able to find one easily and pick it up for pence. "Sunday caramel sweetheart hair / Flowerdew meathook sunshine flare." For my money one of the sweetest couplets of the whole C86 era.

Okay, I'm prepared to admit the Yanks came in many good flavours, too. Get with the raving likes of The Crawdaddys, The Lyres, Chesterfield Kings, Fleshtones, Gravedigger V, The Unclaimed, Salvation Army, and fucking die!

But! If you want the English antidote, lemme hip you to The[e] Milkshakes, instead of the Creation-born and what's known as C86, cos they were the ones doing the dirty fighting against the menace of rock bores in the shape of yer Greyn on Reds, Thyn Whyte Ropes, Long Ryders and other assorted shytes, like The Fuzzytones. And although Thee Milkshakes lost the battle, they won the war. From Chatham, even. See, that's where Billy Childish came from, already.

McNuggets

The other day I was trawling through a slew of old e-mails, tutting over the state of my bulging sack, when what should I come across but a post from the Bomp newsgroup about the new Children of Nuggets box set? It's in its early days at the moment, and although the track-listing is strong in parts, like the bodybuilder's egg, it's looking fairly shabby in others, with many repeats from various nonentity bands and US bias that kind of negates the real hidden history of what was happening back in the retro day.

The whole point about the Nuggets thing is that there was more to US garage rock than LA in the 1960s. That's why they did the extended box set, and then Vol. II. And even in the 80s the garage rock scene was US-wide and worldwide, with bands springing up from LA to the Arctic Circle, via Greece, Yugoslavia-as-was, Oz, Leicester — you name it.

The early track-listing looks okay-ish, with a flavour of what was going on 60s-wise in the mid-80s, but there are about 20 double entries from individual bands, which means that the public are getting 20 fewer genuine rockin' obscurities for their money. I'm here to tell yez there was loads to choose from back then.

I'm dismayed that the utterly stinky Smithereens are included, as are the — Ahem! — Inspiral Carpets. Okay, so they've also comped a fair number of my faves mentioned above, but rather than give the world the Shamen and Jesus and Mary Chain, true psych-pop by any measure, what do do get? The Revolving Paint Dream and Biff! Bang! Pow! Duh!!!

I'm totally stoked that Hove's own Vibrasonic made it on to the list. Vic Fitch is long overdue some big respect. And The Green Telescope are there, too. Go, Lenny Helsing! And the DMZ's "Busy Man": "Yow! Have some mo'! Need some mo'! I'm not yer busy man!"!!! Let's see if all the good stuff is still there when Children of Nuggets hits the record stores. We'll see what happens when this shit hits the fans!!!

It's like I've always said, once the fans become the scenesters, watch out for totalitarianism of the rockin' kind!! They'll try and control yer mind!!! Disobey!! Always do it the wrong way!!!!!

Missin' Links
An Occasional Column

In an excited moment last week I sussed that there was a similarity between the atmospheric rainy interludes on Neu's Neu and the ones on Mickey Newbury's Frisco Mabel Joy (Elektra, 1968). What was the link? I bit my already ragged lip (Note to single self: ladies prefer moist lips to dry ones) and trawled my archive.

Obviously, Newbury did his military service in Europe but not, to my knowledge, in the land of sausage and pickled cabbage. He was stationed in England the whole time and ended his stay here in Swiss Cottage, London, of which he retained fond memories.

During their time together Neu may or may not have discovered the delights of the man Minnsy calls "The Newbs", but like all men, on hearing him once they'd have found something to grok in his discuses. And being German they would certainly appreciate his Romantic tendency to sweep through time, space and interlinked personal experiences in the course of a single song.

But the vital link evades me! I've lost the thread. Oh, Ariadne!!!! I'm left thinking about the connections between Neu's and Erik Satie's use of tension and fragile melody. But that's for another time.

After the elation of my elliptical discovery wore off and I'd had a cuppa, I was then drawn to thinking that it might actually be the sound of the sea, in which case those krafty Krauts must have lifted the whole thing from Quadrophenia. Either that or they made it up themselves.

Reviews
A Cormorant For Punk n Rock

It seems that the rumour about local types, The Shades of Meaning, planning a whole LP's-worth of shinola, with the excellent working title of "Seven Shades of Meaning", was more than a little wrong. So we'll all be waiting for this "utterly regenerative creative spout" (it sed there! — RH.) till Hull freezes under.

Anyway, the Shades's two cassingles are included on the Brighton compilation, Complete Cormorant Cassingles, 2004-2004, which is to be bunged out soon by the mighty Cormorant. Closely followed by a review in these pages, if I can keep up.

As the name suggests, the Cormorant cassingles LP contains the full roster of releases on the sadly, and let's face it totally understandably, defunct cassette-only mini-label that lasted for two months at the end of last year. We await this new local product with bated breath, and enthusiasm.

Local Graverobber Caught on CCTV

I've a mate who works as a CCTV operator. It's not a bad life. Imagine T S Eliot's Tiresias patching together his favourite moments for private hard-drive consumption in the privacy of his own bath. If you can't imagine that, think of something else. In fact, even if you can, don't. Anway, I've told him he'd better watch it. Look at the trouble those NCP boys got into with their car park sex DVD. Although that was a public service, if you ask me. They should be taken up Bartholomews by the Gay Mayor and given tea and medals.

Where was I? Ah, yes! Ever wondered how the Brighton poster men make their money? This chap's provided me with evidence, as if any were needed, of where the profit comes from in the sordid job of promoting. Is it possible that a man aware of the arcane politics of the International Gravediggers could himself become a graverobber?

Picture the scene. On a dark, windy, rain-swept hill overlooking old Brighthelmstone, a Dickensian figure in a Crimean War-era hospital orderly's tunic trudges up to St Nicholas's Church, shovel over one shoulder and canvas gas mask case over the other. He surveys the pitch black for witnesses and gets down to business.

In the murkiest corner of this midnight churchyard, hunched against the wet dark and totally immersed in his solitary, charnel labour, the tousle-headed figure first removes the loosened turves from an unmarked grave, then digs down further and stuffs handsful of A3 and A5 sheets into the hole. Finally, his dark work ended, he purses his moist, brandy-sodden lips, makes the sign of the wanker & departs as swiftly as he came.

How many dreams has this man buried? How many bands and club-runners have gone to the grave dreaming fretfully of full houses and adoring fans? "Where are all the people?" the DJs and girls and boys in the bands ask, questioning the grey morning skies now emptied of God and hope. "Did we not make our posters eye-catching, new and lovely?"

One can only imagine the depths of his depravity. How many graves has he despoiled? How many ancient, gangling skeletons in this fair town are going to glory detourned, like so many unwitting low-rent pharoahs, by colour-photocopied collages done by Miss Pain, or those awfully nice chaps from It Came from the Sea?

Obviously, there's no money in postering these days. Well, there's only so many sites to cover. And people only bother reading the ones in the Heart and Hand anyway. You might as well chuck the rest away...

Following several phone calls by my chum to others in the local surveillance trade, there are rumours of similar footage from Shoreham Harbour, but at the time of printing these are as yet unconfirmed.

Top Funny-Men Of English Rock 'n' Roll

No. 1: Mark Lamarr

What a cunt he is. Sitting there with his finger on the rectal pulse of pop culture, up his arse. Big mates with Phil Jupitus. Two cunts. And Bill Bailey. Two cunts and a prick. Now, in my book you've got the makings of a half-decent joke there about the makings of a half-decent movie. But the BBC actually go ahead and make another series of Never Mind the Buzzcocks, which isn't either.

Funny guy. Got loads of records from the golden olden days. Let's listen to him blowing the fluff off his needle...

This is the man who got Thee Headcoats on to do a session for him in the mid-90s, when he was sitting in for Mark and Lard when they did the late night show on Radio 1, then got huffy when his fave band didn't show the proper appreciation for him doing them such a big favour.

Being a funny guy, he forgave the band and tried to make things better-and by doing so presumably hoped to form some sort of back-slapping English rock 'n' roll humour heritage association-by-shmoozing backstage at a Headcoats gig sometime afterwards. Johnny Johnson, Thee Headcoats' former bass player, was chuckling merrily as he told me that they weren't having it, and the funniest man in rock 'n' roll was faced with around 80-something combined years of Medway-born horrorshow malice-banter which reduced the cunt virtually to tears. Now that's funny.

Bad Luck Town

Hey, you lot!! It's been a while!! Letsagettabittarockin'! One time!!

The year started with me and Jim "Sonic" Smith moving to the far East for our collective health. Getting old and oiled is no f**king joke. So we rented a fabulous apartment in Hastings, overlooking the smoke-houses and there we made a start on Smithy's autobiography, "From Born Bad to Worse", chronicalling the years and the tears of his love affair with the showbiz highlife.

Unfortunately, it all went a bit Suzy Wong and we split up. Yes, the rumours are true!! We went gay!! So what? It's 2005 and the hole world's queer. Anyway, he's gone back to birds and I've gone to ground in Hove with my collection of vintage jazz mags. I keep swearing I'll never live in Hove again, and this is the fourth time I've moved back. Hove is always nearer than you think.

You'll have sussed that this is a bit of a stop-gap ish, due to reduced circumstances and me being on pills for me nerves/living in me car, etc. Needless to say, we'll be back to the full gamut of sherry-induced mayhem sooner than you can say "Spunk"!!! Finally, thanks to the lovely chap/chappess known only as Z, who mailed me and flatteringly described me as the Thomas Carlyle of rock.

Keep it free!!
Hugs and XXXs,
Your Editor

19

September 2005
Post-Punk Special

Brighton, 26th September 2005
The Day Taste Broke

I wandered out into daylight to get a wholemeal loaf and some coffee beans, expecting something and nothing to happen. It didn't. But something else a lot less interesting did.

As a mincing self-confessed phile-ing cabinet, I'm used to braying in aid of arguments pertaining to antiquarian sounds too frail and elderly to make it into most people's ears and much too filthy for most people to finger through. But even I, a veteran of the retro era and usurper of the common sense and historicism usually invoked to validate revisionism, was revolted at the spectacle of 25 or so teenagers, led by three grown men, mincing through the streets of in favour of a musical taste revival.

Oh yes, it was the day of the long-awaited Brighton Post-Punk March! The flyer advertising this sorry event reads as follows:

WE WON!
SO GIVE YOURSELF A MEDAL!
WEAR IT WITH PRIDE!
THE ROCKISTS SAID IT WASN'T
PROPER ROCK 'N' ROLL!
THE PUNX SED IT WAS TOO
INTERLLECTUAL!
THEY ALL SAID IT WAS TOO
BORING!
BUT WE WON!

And there they were, some with banners sloganned poorly with modernist saws, others re-appropriating Franco Marinetti for the umpteenth time, still more others handing out homemade 'records' made of liquorice, cardboard and black paper.

One wee man even had the temerity to stop me and ask in French, simpering wildly back to his mates, "Aimez vous disco ou punk rock, grandpére?" I replied, in my best French, "J'aime les haricots, j'aime le sauce, j'aime le relations sexuelles!" Naturally, he failed to appreciate my proletarian lyrical-linguistic pun in opposition to his genre-bound ironic supposition of my taste position. (My beard uncombed, my hair unwashed, I was sashaying along the street wearing the jeans I'd bought when 3 stone lighter and my "I Lyke Psyke 'n' Punke" T-shirt.)

It seems that the jerky guitars and off-centre haircuts have won in the great competition of music taste. Post-punk is back, fronted by Franz Ferdinand, with his 'emotive' Bowie voice. The Detournement crowd in Brighton, thanks to educationalists Jim Smith and Steve Sexton have swept the thicko retro opposition aside and set the world back on its angular axis. I guess they'll not be going back to DJ-ing crappy old 60s tunes now. Oh no!!! When they get bored of Detournement (it's been going three years already), they'll probably rehabilitate Acid House and make a fortune, retire and go to university to get educated properly.

Ce Reprise Qui N'en Est Pas Un

So, post-punk, then. What's it all about? I'm a bit in the dark about this current fuss. Other than it's one of those 20-odd-years-on taste resurge happenings. But don't call interest in post-punk a matter of taste hierarchies or a revival, because those who know will pin you to a wall and tell you it's progressive music made by conscious people. And you can't revive the progressive, because it's already and always progressing.

Oh, come off it! It is a revival, really, isn't it? Only you can't call it one. It's a revival that isn't.

Post-Punk Or Retro? Vote Now!

So what's going on? It's nothing more than a version of the rip-off game of "Who d'you like best?" on daytime TV. Vote now!!! Tommy Steele or PiL? Walls or windows? Up or down? Bird shit or dog shit?

How did we get to a point where post-punk came to be like forgotten psychedelia or something?

Drowning In A Fog Of Word-Breath

I should've known post-punk would be coming back. It's been a long time coming — been a long, lonely time since Elastica.

Its formation and suppression in the late 1970s to early 1980s was the first gleaming of seriousness emerging in popular culture in Britain in a long while. But this scene comprised of people taking themselves too seriously was an ideological response to the 'serious culture' of grotesquely over-entitled elites as targeted by Stewart Home and the Smile gang, among others, during the Art Strike of 1990 to 1993, among other things. Post-punk was a self-contained outburst of the everyday music history fan, borne of the more heroic autodidactism of punk rock.

Most importantly, post-punk was to a great extent music created under erasure. Think Joy Division. If you're thinking for yourself in a world with no models to mould yourself to, you'll probably become over-serious. If no one else will take your opinions seriously, you have to. And you may even go crazy and die trying. Consider Spike Milligan, made mad by not being able to take his funniness seriously. And something similar happened to Ian Curtis. Killed by serious culture. No one ever wore their autodidactism lightly.

Accordingly, due to the autodidactism of its proponents, post-punk also sung about explorations of individualism through historical images and everyday narratives. Joy Division, for instance, set themselves up as if projected upon by ancient newsreels, giving their songs a feel like fresh reportage from the simultaneous past. In one respect, historical music.

On Thinking I Might Have To Like Only What's Available

I missed the point of post-punk first time round, even though I first started getting into music in 1978, and I'm not sure I'm ready to accept the music press hype — then and now. There was a general feeling of "What now?" in the aether between 1978 and 1979 that manifested itself in bands and music writers invoking art and literature, and music thoughts other than rock n roll ones, in aid of their works.

I could see and hear the differences in the forms of songs, with increasing use of caesura and syncopation, for example, and between bands with a group mentality and those with an alternative idea of branding their sounds at a time when picture sleeves were a big deal. Magazine was clearly a different beast from the Buzzcocks. But I was rolling with the changes and using the differences to navigate by.

I came to know all about post-punk, because that's what they were calling it in Sounds and the NME. Generally speaking I didn't like music as a thing in itself, and I wasn't interested in labels being attached to sounds, but I liked listening to tunes and hearing them as if at random, whenever the radio was on and when I was round friends' places with records and tapes being played. If I was into anything, I was into individual tunes. And I was more into the sounds bands made, hand crafting their feelings with industrial tools, than I was into particular kinds of bands or one band in particular. Except I liked the The Damned a lot — but even there it was the first album, "Damned, Damned, Damned", that got to me.

I was worried that, having missed out on punk rock and not liking the thing that was replacing it, I might have to start liking what was available. The thought was terrifying. My hair stood on end. Etc. I distinctly remember listening to the radio in 1979 and wondering which tunes I should like.

It didn't take long for me to make my mind up. I liked plain-sung/spoken vocals, melodies, hooks and arrangements, like those in Joy Division's "Atmosphere" and Young Marble Giants' "Radio Silence", that altered the very ecology.

I didn't like cod-reggae guitar stabs — although I heavily dug reggae and dub then, and still do — and I hated jerky effect-ridden funk, singers with overblown 'emotive' 'soul' voices and muso bullshit.

Given my likings, it came as something of a relief to hear bands concentrating on making individual tunes. PiL were great, Joy Division, as I've mentioned already, were beyond great, verging on fucking brilliant. The Fall were funny and terrifying. The Dead Kennedys were inexplicably nailed down in political presentism masquerading as dystopic counter-futurism and they had a great sound.

You better believe I was listening under erasure. And I liked the good stuff.

But what of the competition in that brave new beat era. Yes, folks, the bands still had guitars, basses and drums. Not so 'post', then, these punks... Echo and The Bunnymen didn't move me much. I loathed The Teardrop Explodes due to the quality of Julian Cope's voice. I liked a couple of The Psychedelic Furs' singles, but I finally saw them play in 1984 and was revolted by their overblown rock-star drivel. Thinking back, it's strange, given my past/present preference for guitars, that I noticed and dug the dark, electronic, confessional and sexual underside of post-punk, best done by The Passage, Suicide and Soft Cell, more than the stuff bunged out by the jerky guitar bands.

Modernarianism
From Modernism To Modernist Populism To Popular Modernism

In an exciting cultural twist, punk rock, which burst out of the transatlantic metropolitan music scene to the provinces in 1976 through 1977, had itself became a culture of the provinces.

The impact of post-punk bands revealed how intensely the punk rock experience had changed Britain's music cultures; it also emphasised the long-lasting effect of the counterculture in Britain — focused in art schools and informed by consciousness of the transformational potential in re-appropriating past movements, like Dada, Futurism, Surrealism, Fluxus, and the rest — which persisted in youth-oriented music culture even though the musical and general cultural earth had supposedly been scorched by 'proletarian' punk rock.

However, let's not promote post-punk to a position of highness in a bygone cultural hierarchy, imposing a high/low dualism based on supposed opposites that actually exist, play and affect each other simultaneously in space and sometimes in time.

How far can we get by invoking the grotesque or pulp in opposition to a monolithic 'serious' culture and setting one against the other? I prefer to view cultures as simultaneous discourses. I don't want to listen to stuff I don't want to listen to. Surely an effective and affective version of an idea, whether regarded as pulp or proper, is a discursive rejoinder. Do we still have to define political positions to things and assign taste judgments based on a supposedly empowering trash aesthetic? I don't want to do that. So I'm not going to.

Referring back to the modernists of the past, I've read Freud, Eliot, Pound, Lovecraft and Buchan, all of whom were aware of the others' works, whether they mention them, and I regard all of them as participants in the creation of modern culture, whether they were/are regarded as Modernists. I don't want to keep on having to narrate Lovecraft as a "pulp modernist" or whatever. Writing in the present, his work was modern, even if his antiquarianism set him against fashion.

Accordingly, if I were asked to name my favourite post-punk band from the early-80s hyperthetically, I'd say "The Milkshakes".

From Counterculture To Multicultures

And despite the influence of reggae and dub on music post-punk, we're stuck with Franz Feckin Ferdinand. So much for The Specials. So much for "the post-punk drive for a reinfusion of blackness", which someone once claimed to be the case. So much, then, for UB40. Can you believe that there were people in 1980, in the middle of a massive international depression with record unemployment, who didn't even know what UB40 meant?

Let's widen the perception of post-punk to include other popular post-punks. But what are the chances of that happening if modernism — for Pete's sake! — continues to be represented by an oppositional discourse between the high/serious and the low/grotesque?

Neither Ventriloquism Nor Mummery

Started by art school graduates and students aware of its prole-potential, then snatched away by the proles themselves, later punk rock — hardcore punk for punx — became a focus for affective disaffection, not necessarily in opposition to post-punk acts of sensible beauty. And being in the hands of the people, who were enjoying versioning it in their image, punk rock became a less desirable commodity.

Post-punk became the new urban sound for aspirational provincial types with brains, as punk had been before it. However, centralist music journalism required metropolitan-based sounds, because that's where the industry was located (London and Manchester). The fact of its disappearing off the popular radar, unlike punk rock which persisted, tells its own story.

The bits of post-punk that made it out to the provinces and stayed in the aether were the bits that mattered: the funk of bands like the Gang of Four and the ever-awful Shriekback and the tribal drums of Adam and the Ants, Killing Joke and Southern Death Cult, among others. But the funk had never really gone away. The 'smoothies', for example, — where I grew up in Cambridgeshire, in the mid 1970s and early 80s, the clean-cut sworn enemies of all punk rockers, queers and anyone not a smoothie — were listening to soul, disco and all things black all along.

X And Y Unite And Fight!

Amidst the increasing opportunities for independent record distribution, punk and post-punk bands were, from 1980 onwards, competing for sales in the newly formed independent chart.

The Apocalypse Punk Tour of 1981, named after an ongoing attempt in Sounds to define the early 80s hardcore punk scene, brought together bands — Discharge & The Exploited were the big names — with a more or less nihilistic take on punk rock, which was proletarian, but not altogether lumpen, and political, although not always conscious. In fact, it was a indicator that people were making life choices based on music made by bands. For the first time, large groups of itinerants were following bands around the country.

The 1981 Christmas on Earth event in Leeds was the first punk rock festival in Britain. It was massively successful, even three long years after the Sex Pistols packed it in. And a year is a long time in punk rock — much longer than a year in these late days of retro, which seem to go on for longer and longer but with less effect.

But were the hardcore punx as grotesque as they should not doubt have liked to be regarded? Was their voicing themselves a carnivalesque episode or an act of discursive engagement? Or both. With a laugh on the side.

Discharge, the band for whom Apocalypse Punk was named, had internalised anti-nuclear and anti-state discourses to such an extent that their being as a collectivity and their recorded works produced a unitone monolith of protest, although their effect was much more interesting than their intentional simplicity. Discharge's song titles, including "You Take Part in Creating the System", "Two Monstrous Nuclear Stockpiles" and "Maimed and Slaughtered", need no explanation, then or now. There's little room for doubting that Discharge were offering reflexive responses, documenting in a slow rolling news format the degradation of representational politics and the concomitant rise in opportunities for self-representation despite the former.

The other bands on the Apocalypse tour were less effective rhetoricians, but showed the extent to which punk rock as a thing beyond music genres had provided a space for inspired, clever and energetic people without publishers to vocalise their concerns and revealed the extent to which people without social or cultural entitlement, through gaining a university or polytechnic degree, could say something to an audience and put the hurt on their narrative targets.

Lest we forget, the hardcore punk scene, like post-punk, was also a fruitful place for women to express themselves in music. Although that's not to say that sexism wasn't rife. Bur there may have been a bit less in punk rock circles.

On that tack, in the early 90s I read an interview with one of the ladies from Huggy Bear, who said that one of the elements of Riot Grrrl was about getting women to expropriate the space at the front at gigs. I clearly recall swearing and burning the offending music paper, as I remembered seeing young women fighting for space at the front at hardcore punk concerts. And she had obviously never attended a performance of the Sex Gang Children, followed by a horde of aggressive teenage women and girls who actively possessed the places they played. Her Punk, empowered as it undoubtedly was, was not the only punk, as many women would have told her, had she asked or even thought about it for a bit.

Folk Radicalism Chord Change

It's right to view engaged post-punk artistes, notably the Pop Group and the Gang of Four — and The Fall, and loads of others, including some of the hardcore punk bands, come to think of it — as exponents of a kind of folk radicalism. Live music cultures were the pulse of political activity in the late-70s and early to mid 80s, Rock Against Racism being the most well known. That's where the political action was. And many of those involved had taught themselves all they knew about music and politics, not to mention art and literature. Which I won't.

Beyond party politics, Discharge and Joy Division were engaging locally at a time when political internationalism was the arena in which the fashionable were activising. In the long term, and globally, the creation and maintenance of radical ecologies can be seen to be happening everywhere. But in the short term, and locally, it's the voices nearer to home that speak the loudest, and anything else sounds like ventriloquism. Listen to the voices.

Anyway, I dint like being told how to feel by political types. And I hated even more being told how to connect together the stuff I liked. The whole Movement movement thing gave me the creeps.

Past-Foward

I gave up on contemporary music fashions in 1982 at 16, after I realised that psychobilly was a music fashion too far, and started pursuing antiquarian sounds and listening to contemporary pop music and punk rock all at the same time. By doing so, I relinquished by default any claim I'd had on identity, and I've had nothing to do with identity since then.

I'd found that then unfashionable old musics had thrown up sounds and tunes at least as interesting as those being made during my youth. The new punk rock and skinhead bands of the early 1980s were churning out some really fiery tunes. Pop music was also a lot of fun. Joe Meek had made already made loads of exciting pop records. So had many other bands in the 1960s, in the UK and the US. GBH were fusioning metal and punk and the Bad Brains had exploded the whiteness of punk and given it a new fastness.

It seemed I was more into the long-term — past/future — than the more fashionable short term. Distancing myself and mixing sounds obsessively, I was becoming a version.

And that's that.

Next time

More about the boredom/repetition nexus. Plus reviews of re-releases, including in-depth sideways and lengthways looks at Odysseus and The Herdge and Phil's Phellers!!

Gitsum!
Your Editor

20

October 2005

"I propagate British cultural depravity"
— Mr Pendlebury, *The Lavender Hill Mob*

Hey there, buddy? What is all this?

Everyone wants to know what I'm up to. Sure, I get praise heaped on me, but I also get the questions. Always with the questions! Ever since the Hunter's voluntary, unpaid, excellent and talented Webstress set up your No.1 Site for Rare Rock 'n' Roll (Which I ruined, failed to maintain and finally couldn't afford to keep — RH), I've been bombarded with e-mails, some of which have even not offered me out!!

My finest achievement was my little ole site getting linked to from Ugly Things, the granpappy of modern archive-rockin'!! Any poor souls will now get a 404 for they efforts!!! Must mail to apologise sometime.

In other news, I've been asked to lecture at the ICA!!! Yes, my fine fellows!!!! I got the e-mail summons just t'other day. "Come and tell us about your toons", they said. Yeah, yeah. Just another unconfirmed guest, I guess. I'll let you know how I get on... One kind soul has been kind enough to call me the Thomas Carlyle of Rock! Like... whom?!?! And another's likened me to William Hazlitt!! (Personally, I've no time for that ghastly mess of unidentifiable animal parts and secret spices — Mmmmm, RH) Frankly, I'm holding out for likenings to people with a bit more "Go" to em, if you know what I mean! I've been waiting, but ya'll ain't doing me that way.

Be that as it may, I'm still doing it my way Thanx to no funkin' body but me! I've been doing you like this for a whole lotta long time. And I still ain't even gotta licence!!!

Whatever. The majority of people are simply asking me what the hell I think I'm doing!! Well, gather round and I'll tell the tell and say the say of the story of what it is, this here.

For those of you who don't get it — you poor souls whose sore lack o' Hep means ya don't know The Unwritten Rule — Rockhunter is many things. It's "A Canticle for Liebowitz" of rock n roll. It's The Forgotten in search of The Unknowns. It's the global newspaper of my state of mind. Gibber. It's the local music paper of yesteryear, replaying the The Past to those who are doomed to repeat it. It's bait for eedjit wannabe celebrockers ceaselessly repeating tedious quasi-experiential factoids. We're audacious and facaetious, just like Spurs. Fuggedabowdit!

This ain't retro re-enactment any more, people, we're in a new era of real, not ersatz. Living-being, not homage. Ring the Alarm! As the sounds die, we're gathering up the slack. We're reconstructing the f-f-forgotten obvious!!!

In military terms, detachments, and independent companies for that matter, are spin-off options to deal with specific ad hoc problems that can't be dealt with by ordinary means. We're talking proaction, close targeting and collusion. My detachment is similar, albeit a personal response to things in general.

Where was I? Oh yeah, it's the plain-speaking magazine for the plain people of Brighton 'n' Hove, this young Metromonolith. And the free folk of the whole World.

It's for people who live lifestyles that are worthless, worn, shallow and repetitive in their ceaselessness, as they grasp for the declassé elements that will subsume them within a wider mass of more valuable experiences, othering their own moribund aspirationalism. It's like a car for your hands. Or somesuch idiot new-language marketing phrase.

Right, enough of what they sneeringly describe as 'Vision' — revolutionary capital's least agreeable attempt at the anulment of dreams — and on with the Motley. And that's "Hall", rather than "Crüe", olden TV comedy fans. Are you with me?

Let's get 'em, you fellows!!!!
Your Editor

21

SEPTEMBER 2006

TUNNEL RIFFING

Right then, where was I? Over the past few years, I've had innumerable inquiries about the lost art of tunnel riffing. What does this phrase mean? Who was doing it? And when? Where did it come from? Why has it been forgotten? I'd like to take this opportunity to lay this hoary subject to rest, once and for all.

Well, during the days of the 'post-punk against rockism' debate in the early 1980s, few intelligent voices could heard above the hubub of shitbag drivel in the Ism Factory (a vile Stasi-contemporary wilderness, where good tunes were abolished and you had to have bummed the corpse of God to be allowed admission — RH), and there were still fewer intelligent dissenting opinions offered up against the assertion that rock was the problem and post-punk was the (final) solution to the rock problem.

Tony Wilson's version of modernism was a laff-riot — serve up Situ-actions as a Marxian final solution to the cultural problem of fun. Yeah, alright already, Anthony. We got it!!

Christ! Some berks still think there's mileage in the Wilson's analysis. There's myriad webspace devoted to the moribund culture-thread called 'post-punk' that dares not evoke 'rockism' for fear of it rising to devour them. And in these revisionist days, one could actually be forgiven for thinking that post-punk won. See them all pouting a bit too self-consciouly, wrapping their messy-prissy hair round their noggins one more time, like so many Bobby Charltons, then sashaying louchely around the revolving door of the dismal club scene. They're too busy collecting their clever-medals to see the future coming on like a hungry ogre. Anyway, who cares? Such obvious nonsenses have to be fought against, but this is not the time or place to do so. (We'll be having a word about this in the not-too-distant future — RH)

Anyway, as bad as it was then, it wasn't even half as bad as it is now, in these latter days of Lore-Bore mags — yer Mojos, Uncuts, etc. Gadzooks and forsooth! can it really be 20 years ago, today? Or was it 25? (Enough, already, of this gay folderol, back to the subject in hand!! — RH)

Lest we forget, the early 80s were also the time of NWOBHM, when the Iron Maidens, Girlschools and Witchfinder Generals stalked this fair land of Albion, wielding their Axes of Evil (I wrote that when it was topical and funny — RH). It's hard to say how the likes of yourn Bauhaus's, Joy Division's, Virgin Prunes's, or Scritti Politti's ever came to rule the roost of retrospection, amidst the cacophony of metal grinding against metal, but that's lifestyle choices for you. That's a wake-up call!!! Must get round to my Roots of Goth special, as promised in the pub last year. Ho blemmin' hum.

So, there we were, all confused after Johnny Rotten decided to flaunt his Bowie trousers in PiL, with punk going national in dayglo and the provinces fighting back in black, when lo and behold!, who should appear on the parapets, with one eye on the football results and another on the treasure trove of Britain's riff-heavy musical past? Enter the Cockney Rejects, the lost link missing between punk and rock, in whom lived the canny proletarian gifts of vulgar wit and self-worth.

Now, Steve Jones had boogied the Pistols into the charts with his string-damping technique lifted right off the Chris Spedding versions of his own riffs. (And that's a recursive conundrum that I really can't be bothered to go into!) It's a fact that the early punkers preferred the Stooges-style open-attack rhythm riffs. Check out the

Fen-edge favourites The Users for a right old Stoogian death-river racket. But that's as maybe. See, my view is Spedding was only doing what came natural after his years on the blues-in-a-basket circuit in the pubs, rocking, like. Pub rock was more than just self parody. Imagine versioning your own stuff at the same time as actually playing it! OK, so Lee Perry was doing it all over the place already, but Jonesy, via Spedding, was doing it culture-jam style!! I reckon Lydon couldn't believe his luck when he saw the power of Version running through Jones's guitar-playing and, as soon as he'd had a listen to Jah Wobble's ragged-arsed dub collection, he did "2+2" and went "4"! And that's where post-punk started, with self-Version. But as I said, I really ain't having this conversation.

Okay, so there was the Rejects, bouncing off the walls with bathtub speed, terrace chants, Nazareth and all sorts of other hard rock nightmares inside their branes. They'd got into the punk sound by mistake, thinking the Pistols were a boogie band, which of course they were, but no one else knew it yet, that's all. Everyone else was loving the Punk Rock hype! They saw right thru!! Like the Small Faces before them — small of stature, working class, own little world — the Rejects got all excited and done themselves a favour by transforming and accelerating the sound they loved. You could say they went amplic. Of which more a little later.

All right? That's where it started. Gary Bushell, Jimmy Pursey and that ended up producing the boys after EMI gave them some studio time. Enter the most powerful guitar sound ever — the best use of string damping in rock, in my humble fucking opinion. Bar none. Not even Sabbath. This is one better; it's like Black Sunday, if you will (if you take Sabbath to refer to the Saturday, as me and the Hebrews do).

Lest not forget that Bushell was, with Ross Halfin, one of the faces of NWOBHM, nor that the Rejects were in with all the same gang. These youngsters were doing punk through a heavy rock filter. They'd Sabb-otaged the Sex Pistols' trademark sound, the wee scamps!

So, firm-handed as you like, the West Ham riff-raff offloaded a job lot of riffs in a raffish manner. They'd stumbled upon the one artefactual sound-motif that could encapsulate their understanding of what the rock was going on! In doing so, they led myself, and possibly many others, to scurry off looking for more of the same, only to be disappointed. For theirs was the one of a kind! Years later, perhaps foolhardishly, I linked their monomaniac ur-power-chords with Isidore Isou's concept of lettrisme. Of course, having done so, I needed a critique of this flawed analysis of materialist culture-streaming. I'm still looking!!

Excuse me if I've misunderstood Asger Jorn's statement:

"It is time to become aware of the drawbacks of all the systems of perspective derived from classical geometry. Many errors arise from a major illusion of modern savants: a distinction between 'classical' and 'modern' geometry was made in the belief that the autonomy of classical geometry could be saved, and that it could be taught as geometry and that which had superseded it were simultaneously true. In the geometry of Euclid, and this has been transmitted to the non-Euclidean systems, the point is defined as a spatial location with no spatial dimension. This omits the fact that the point, bereft of spatial dimensions, still represents the temporal dimension, thanks to its duration. The point thus introduces the dimension of time into spatial organisation, which is the basis of a new elementary geometry. (It is this new study of the point which enables the situation to be understood as a spatial-temporal work alien to the old properties of art).

When the point is considered as a pure idea, geometry is infected with metaphysics and lends itself to the emptiest constructions of metaphysics. Nothing is left of it." — and I don't think I have — The Rejects, or more specifically, Mickey Geggus, their guitarist, happened upon the pivot-point of rock as they saw it, turning one time-bound artefactual trope into a virtuous moment, thereby possibly consciously realising Isidore Isou's will to assimilate "the innovating truth of the immediate past and present, by openly recognising the forms of future evolution of the aesthetic disciplines that will truly be born for the history of culture and for the place of each author in this history."

Of course, as your man Jorn said, in his critique of the original Lettriste,

'Human creation does not resemble this sort of French garden, such as Isou would want to embellish, the centre of which he believes he will come to definitively occupy, simply because, preaching untiringly in the emptiness, he foresees (in his own words, 'the opening of a new amplic') the completely symmetrical reproduction of the other side of Isou."

So, who was responsible for this lost art, this nigromansiery, this black-handed, Black Sabbatarian last gasp of working class Resurrection Funk? After a second bottle of grog the other night, I recalled, through the Scotche Mystes of Tyme, that me, Rob and Neale were always going on about tunnel-riffing back in the early-80s, only a couple of yeras after the Rejects had done the do. We used to say it was the great lost art of rock 'n' roll, was Mickey Geggus' favourite guitaring methodology: the old string-damping chug-a-lug. I was led to believe by my synapses that tunnel-riffing was promoted way back when in the pages of Sounds by Garry Bushell, an ex-Trot, who, it turned out, had a soft ear for the yesteryear connective factor in pop culture. Presumably, in the Rejects, he found himself unable to withdraw far from his materialist roots and ended up finding a properly proletarian historical moment to work with. Blimey, where did that come from?

Given all that, it should be clear to even the most dimwitted of the current slew of post-punk numbskulls that in making amplic the object and cause of Geggus's desire — string damping a la Sabbath — the Rejects were consciously emptying the rock-sound fabrication industry as much as any of Tony Wilson's supposedly more conscious friends and prole 'finds', who may or may not have been as up on Lettrism as he claims to have been.

Oh, the 1980s!! All bollocks, of course. Just another strand of Bore-Lore.

Imagine the scene, my pretties! On one hand, Tony Wilson, on the other, Bushell — one a pro-situationist, the other a party man. Two materialisms clash. But that really is a fairytale for another time, as Louis Ferdinand Céline said. Phew!

To cut the story even longer. (Bear with him, it's been a long year — RH). I emailed Bushell, who I remembered as the Mush who christened the ensuing racket 'tunnel-riffing'. After all, it was he who invented Oi! after the Rejects's tune, 'Oi! Oi! Oi!' Or was it the other way round? But that's another kettle of.

Imagine to my surprise on opening my Hotmail inbox one fine morning (Mail me, you lot, I kinda like it!!!!!), only to vada a messagette from the Lord o' Oi! Hisself!! Unfortunately, it seemed I'd barked up the wrong journo. Gazza's pithy response said (and I quote verbatim, so history can judge): "Sorry, never tunnel riffed in me life. Are you mixing me up with Deaf Barton?"

Of course! The thot plickens!! Geoff "Deaf" Barton, inventor of the term NWOBHM, Satan's little helper, lover of metal, supporter of Venom, Angel Witch and Diamond Head, Lord High Kreator of Kerrang! The former Sounds man. Could I find Barton's e-mail address so I could ask him? Could I bollocks?!?!

Looks like we'll never know. I, for one, have absolutely no intention of trawling through 1000000000000000000 back issues of Sounds, looking for references. If you know anyone who's that way inclined, get em to write in on a postcard, addressed to someone who gives a toss!!

So, tunnel-riffing it was, is and ever shall be. Arseholes!!

All the beast,
Your Editor

22

September 2006

Antiquarianism, Fictional History, Tradition, Novelty And Beating Collectomania

Very much as in the 15th to 16th centuries, when it was possible to possess and know all the things ever written, in these days of CD reissues of everything, we've reached a similar turning point in history. Previously, the sort of knowledge bunged out on countless rekkids, the Comps of Ages, belonged to the collectors in their dark holes, those strange shadowy beings with no noses. But how did they smell? Bloody awful!!! Some things never change. I diverge...

These comps accumulated just as hidden knowledge, or the occult, if you will (Or even if you won't!!! — RH), was collected and known only to the mouth-breathing self-styled Collecto-Mages of yester-yore. I'm overblowing this a bit, just for effect!! Even the most whiney media studies tosser would have to agree, in retrospect, that collecting — especially in the area of psych/punk — is intensely contextual, even revisionist. Remember, we collectors and enthusiasts were the ones who changed the world by putting value on out-of-date sounds. And God help us for transvaluing forgotten shit!!!!

Woooooaaah! Back to the forge!!! Let's face it, the Renaissance boyos were collectors, with their old documents, wunderkammers and such, but they called themselves alchemists because that's got the buzz of a sexy quest about, while collecting is anything but.

So, the old toons are dead. Rrrring the alarm! ! Another sound is always dying, somewhere. But the Old Ones are being reanimated and all of us are now summoning the gluey voices of the long-dead lost. Even their absence, their much deserved rest, can't prevent them from helping with our digressionarily dubjective historicist inquiries. Even The Unknowns, on Unknown Unknowns Vol. IX........

Julian Cope Is Not The Only Antiquarian

Listen up, you sods!!! You might just learn something. I've spent too many years in the dank, sweaty Basement of Cool, interrogating emptied-out ash-piles and the void, blackened skulls of forgotten keening youths. Plus reconstructing oeuvres from tropic shopping lists. Nigromansiery, they called it, way back when chatting to brazen heads was all the go. But whether the hands were black because of working with dusty old shit, or the hands claimed the title because of the evil they did, or not, is not recorded.

I'd made the mistake of thinking more music was better music. I got myself strung out on plenty. Which sometimes is just not enough. Now, I've always dabbled, getting into a bit of Reggay, Cajun, Country, or whatever strikes my gaze when I'm a bit bored in the Blighty's manifold disc emporia. But I'd went too far and forgot the most important thing — the modus operandi by which I'd worked for all the years when music was the only thing between me and cutting out of this here. Deep knowledge. Or obsession. Either.

I went back to listening umpteen times to the ones that grabbed me. To get them in mi brane. So, without much anew, I hot-footed it back to The Past. I'm still time travelling there most every day. Recent synpase-shifters from the past 18 months include: "Nightmare" by the Gas Company, Mickey Newbury's "How Many Times Must the Piper be Paid for His Song?", Bod Dylan's "Baby,

Let Me Follow You Down", Betty Harris' feedfront epic "There's a Break in the Road"s. That sort of thing. Is it Deep Knowledge, obsession, or competence, that makes me an effective force in the Realm of Rockin?!?!

Basically, to cut a short story a whole lot longer, I've had to work out another way of loving my music. See, although compulsive necrophilia is all very well, a chap needs to feel a pulse every now and then!! As my pal the poet Alan Hay says, nostalgia's a young man's game. Actually, thinking about it, he may have got that off me. See what I mean about all this sorting of things into proper places. Anyway, where was I?!?!

I discovered that, with some age to me, I'd reborn myself as a speculative archaeologist! Like a big ole Graham Hancock of Rock!! And this was my dig!! And it was freaking me out!!! Like, Thensville!!!! I was in an era comparable with the 16th century, when The Past was mostly unwritten on cartloads of crumbly documents with old writing on them and the antiquarian gang decided to find a new way of dealing with The Past, what with all the stuff written about it coming out of the woodwork. It was at that point that John Selden and some of his friends up and down the length of England dumped their wigs on their leathery study tables, alongside old prehistoric flint tools and such, mopped their stubbly, wrinkled heids, sniffed a bit due to the mouldy old parchment dust up their hooters and got weaving with their quills, scritchy-scratchilode on the lamb-chop parchimoult.

What the antiquarians came up with was brilliant! They hit upon the wheeze of putting the olden days documents in date order and tracing back through them to work out who was writing about who. And what. Previously, old papers had been gathered around particular places, or in bundles to prove individual legal cases (who owned that bit of land; who had the right to go hither and yon, or thusly, etc.). No one had thought you could use documents to build a massive picture, rather than focus on detail, using wordy precedents microscope-like. Why, it was almost like painting individual figures in a mural and watching them grow into a representative scene, with the big ones at the front and all the tiny wee fellows in the distance. Not that perspective or a written tradition is the end of the story in either case, but, you know....

Anyway, here's the thing. They'd decided that, at some stage, The Past had grown into The Present, rather than both things having existed all at the same time in different myth-eras all along. Oh, do try and keep up! It was then they found they'd created more of a problem than a solution. How on God's good Earth were they to deal with new documents that came along? There was no end to all the new history they'd allowed to be created with their antiquarian master-stroke!! They'd gone and created Novelty as well as Tradition. And it seems that, at the same time as the wigged ones were about their historical fictions, they were also creating false divisions between 'fiction' and 'history' that would last for at least 500 years. And that's another reason why poor old Copey ain't as original as people seem to think he is. He's no right to call himself a modern antiquarian. Let's all create more fictions from The Past without his implicit permission!! We are all antiquarians, every day of our listening lives.

Right, well. There was I, with a fixed view of how all this music I loved worked, and more of it coming at me every day through comps, downloads, old cassettes turning up down the backs of sofas, and every which way. But I was bored fitting all the new genre toons into the slots I had ready for em. I was sick fed up of waiting, squatting like a perverted wicket keeper!!! "Dear oh dear", I thought, "I've had enough of this. Let's have a read of a book or something."

Anyway, I'm all right now, which is the main thing.

See ya!!!!
Your Editor

23

September 2006

Gaiety Riot

Well, the rumours are true. No more Bad Promoter!! The Miltonian Satan of Provincial Punk (That's me!! — RH) has convinced the Only True Descendent of the Counter-Culture, and Favourite Child of the Lord of Rock 'n' Roll, that if his Heavenly Master had not intended him to escape the Hellish oubliette of Ignorance and Decency, he would have heightened the walls and strengthened the chains. Book One, Paradise Lost. It'll not take ye's long to get up to speed.

In short, me and Jim "Sonic" Smith, the Winking Uncle and Shepherd of Local Rock 'n Roll, the once notorious übersexual self-styled "Jism Magnate", who it's rumoured once piped his excess white man-gravy straight into the national spunk grid, have come to an understanding.

He's carving out a new role for himself as a stubborn stain on Brighton's young-obssessed, at-all-costs positive, brand-aware face. It's all about expressing creative individuality... yeah, yeah, yeah, yeah, yeah, yeah, yeah. The reply of all-knowing upness shuts down negative discourse in return, or slams the backdoor to relight ignorance, feigning comradeship — indeed, for all friendship is a discursive masking.

Anyway, Smithy's bringing it back to the people, like Kurtz would've done, had he been a real person rather than a fiction. Having escaped incarceration in the prison of synchrony, if only he can avoid the pull of the sunlit uplands of state capitalist propaganda, Kim Jong-Il style, we should be seeing some interesting post-ironic developments in the Brighton undercurrent before too long.

I, for my part, have retired from the slow-mo gak-ridden chum-bucket they call Brighton's clubland. I'm getting back. You'll find me listening to music for pleasure. Not conspicuously in public!! It's pleasure and beauty all the way from here on in!!!! Let the DJs bury the dead sounds! Jim Smith, I salute you!!!

Meanwhile, in Kemp Town, I prepare for greater understanding in the future!!

Fi!
Your Editor

24

September 2006

Pub Rock Compendium

I've been inundated with your responses to my articles on pub rock. You lot always cease to amaze me! I've never heard such a lot of old toss spouted by so many sad bastards with a tale to tell!! Thank god I don't drink in pubs any more, I'd forgotted how dismal those places are!!!

Anyway, you've sent in a load of brilliant pub rock band names, some old, some new, that you've found spattered across the expectant, upturned face of the country. It hardly seems worth the effort, since the joke's long since worn off. But I've got a blog to write and forces to multiply. So here they are now :–

Double Yellow Line
Breakin' the Ice
Compos Meantit
Smokey and the Band It
Rain Stopped Play
Can't See the Wood
Slippery Slope
Blues in a Basket
Cause 'n' Effect
Cream of the Crop
2-up 2-down
Train of Thought
Mickey Hart and the Hartbreakers
Street Legal
Hocus Pocus
Rainy Daze
Lager than Life
Wet Weekend
Call Me a Cab
Kangaroo Caught
The Whistle and Flute Band
The Siamese Triplets
The Circuit Breakers
Blues x2
Pot Calling Kettle
Kiss and Tell
Chubby and the Locks

That's quite enough of that. If I never hear another word about pub rock it'll be 1000000000000000 years too soon. Now wash your hands!!

Go now,
Your Editor

25

22 September 2006

Beyond History
Total Nonentities Of Rock 'N' Roll

It used to be a truth universally acknowledged that a man in possession of a shit-load of garage rock records is often in want of a girlfriend. These days, however, if you're a Deep Knowledge Freak, a mouth-breathin' dust-lover, a Grand Groove-Sniffer Pursuivant, you literally can't move for pussy. It's all good!!! I've never had it so much!!!!!

Where was I? As usual, I find myself swamped with a plethora. Actually, that sounds quite nice when you say it aloud. Mmm, I like it! I've been getting my ears around a whole load of recent shite, trying for a little more context. But to be honest it's only the re-releases that're keeping me afloat. And the new comps have been pouring through my letterbox.

Let's get this straight, just so's we're clear, my friends. I'm strictly out of the loop and off the circuit. I got no contacts, brothers and sisters. I don't shmooze. Parties ain't me. I go out and get my records, they don't send 'em to me. Y'unnerstand? So when I open a cardboard mailer, I know it's gonna be something neat. Where's all this heading? Quien sabe, muchachos!! Sono Inglese, yer dig!! I had to get it off me chest!!!

Taking Care Of Your Woollens... And Other Punk Rock Habits

So, what was I least expecting right now?? The return of Woollen Records, that's all!! They always find me!!! How do they find me?? Anyway, good ole Woollen are back with two — count em! — new comps, Fear Us Not, Volumes I & II. But!!! The word in the shop is that the shadowy forces behind this deep underground operation have gone to ground and Woollen has gone, like, totally belly up for the second and final time!! Maybe something to do with the Intellectual Property Squad busting their door in and giving them the ole Ordinary Rendition... off to Nick, that is. Maybe they just didn't pay the bills? Who knows?!? Anyway, let's give credit where it's due, and doff our titfers for the passing of a great rekkid labial.

If you can find any of the super-crazy tri-action spazzola product unleashed by these insaniac punk perverts, buy 'em immediately. You'll never see them again!!!!

My jaw quite literally fell off when I saw the names on the Fear Us Not school register: Dr Fell, The Gaspers, Flash Farm, Trilogy, The Tales of Woad, Avis Savory, The Craftsmen, Gaping Maw, 10-Acre Field, Langston Cove, Angharad, The Oaves, Bent Magician, The Tempus Fugitives, Perfumed Wind, The Sutton Who, dee-da dee-da. And the list goes on and on and on.

Yeah, so we all know about this stuff. I've got a bevvy of these strangeoid concoctions by hook or by crook over the years, but I'm always surprised that anyone else can be bothered. I've absolutely no inclination to go through the process of hawking bootleg comps round the circuit. It's a hamster's wheel, a Sisyphusian task, a knob-ache. Let the other mouth-breathers give themselves hernias. I cannot stress how limited my patience is.

But seriously, both vols of Fear Us Not are pretty nearly totally amazing. And they're virtually giving the things away at a few quid a pop.

Dr Fell's "Beware of yesterday" is the most blustering slab o' psych, with the whoosh and the ping-ing-ing and the wail of Old Tiddy Mun, beckoning the unwary into the dirty magic of the ancient Fens. Oh yes, this is Fen Punk at its best (or F-Punk as its passionate fan calls it). And still the world awaits a wider awareness of this relatively untapped throbbing vein of musical ore. So, you don't dive into the bliss of psych with Dr Fell, you struggle to escape its fenny sucking pit. You don't dig this sort of nutzoid fantasy boogiosity, you syphon it wholesale with a sludge-gulper. Hmm. that's quite enough of that.

The Craftsmen's "Flurries of Heartache" is a workmanlike East Midlands soul epic, nice enough, until... that guitar noise!!! It's a volume pedal waggling, feedfront tour de force!!! Meanwhile, in another part of the Id, I'd like to pit Gaping Maw's "Are you sitting on a map?" against Jason Crest's "Turqouise Tandem Cycle". Paisley handbags at dawn, if you get my drift.

10-Acre Field's "Happy-Go-Lucky" and Langston Cove's "Bank Holiday" are prime examples of how not to write and record your own record in a day. But what a great nightmare!!! Two of the best examples of what I've christened the "1969 Church Hall Sound". Listen and see.

And if you like the rushing sound of a lightning breeze, check Bent Magician's, "Dolly Dangerous", and "It's Her Real Name, She Likes It", the second track by The Craftsmen. "Tempus fugitive" by The Tempus Fugitives is a proper fuzz ripper with, strangely, a complex Scriabin-style 1930s Hollywood filmic interlude. V strange. Back on terra infirma, Perfumed Wind's "Go back to your time" is like gravy on your psychedelic Sunday lunch. Smooth, like...well, like good brown gravy.

Finally, what can I say about "Nuclear Dynamite" by The Oaves? It's a V8 punch in the bollocks. Or quim. They don't discriminate, these fellows. It's 1968, but no one's told The Oaves. Hiding out in a Commer van parked on an allotment in the Vale of Evesham, not knowing the Emperor's surrendered. You get the picture. Think Leviathan's failed TV music career as featured in "A Year in the Life". Imagine if Mike Stewart's Spam had less idea and more volume. Cor!!!

My life is always changed by new toons (new in the Northern Soul sense of the term, mates!!!). I've a collective name for new comps. I call them Nudge-Its. Basically, this refers to a mega- or ur-compilation of arcane tunes you like best, until the next one comes along, or, otherwise, it refers to the love of the last good tune you heard.

Meanwhile, let me go now. I'm getting back into my tape machinery. Cut-ups, making new from old and old from older. Favourite bits of records intertwined Intro+v+c+m8. Mek dem all mix-up. Make something ghastly wonderful. Then imagine what animal it would be if it were one. Actually, I don't think I'm explaining myself too well. So I'll stop now. I shall have a small glass of Marsala. Then a nap, I think.

More new(-ish) comp reviews tomorrow.
Two love,
Yer Editor

26

22 September 2006

The Comp-Post Heap
New Rubbles, Unknown Unknowns, Hubbles and Welsh Rare Beat

Let's get it straight. I'm not interested in cosseting the feelings of musicians or self-styled scene gurus. Including the hang-around cocksuckers who put out comp after comp. It's like DJ-ing. Anyone'd think these creatures invented the tunes they were digging.

Take the New Rubble series. Namely New Rubble, Vol. One, My First Day Without You for starters. This rather shoddy article seems to have been compiled with the value of the comper's own collection at the front of mind. Well, it's his pension, or nest-egg, isn't it? He's been collecting for a zillion years, so why shouldn't he try to get something back for all the hours, days and months he's wasted searching for the ultimate monster earthquake history-killing punk-blues teenage feeback riff-fuck. But what the hey? Why would I wanna waste time putting the fellow down? This comp is chock fulla Beat, the way father used to make it!!! The soundtrack to good times and bad times, this comper's christened his fave sub-genre "CLEANBEAT". Call it what you like, we're heavily into the "Import CD" category here. And I think we all know by now what that means. Let's play safe, people. Radio silence. Code words. Don't give the VAT inspectors or Intellectual Property Spooks anything to go on.

So, New Rubbles, Vol. One is pretty much 2nd string collection territory. It's the sort of stuff you buy for the band name or song title in the hope it'll getcha movin'. We're in the land of the oddly exciting flip to a Big Beat balladeer's career flop. That's the bag. Give it a try. It'll not change your life and you won't have to listen to it more than once. Then you can put it alongside all the other comps you never listen to any more and make a full set.

Now to rubbish New Rubble Vol. 2!!! The drippy hippy who put this mixed bag together opines thusly:

"Prog/psych is a genre generally neglected by singles collectors as the bands of the time were known mainly for their album output rather than their 45s [...] This compilation aims to set the record straight by bringing some of the best examples of the genre to the attention of the afficionados, a timely enterprise as many influential DJs are actively seeking Prog/psych singles to play, exposing them to a wider audience and driving up the price of originals accordingly. Singles such as Taiconeroga's "Speaking My Mind" has recently shot up in the value with others sure to do the same. [...] The value of Prog/psych albums has risen rapidly in the last few years, and 45s are sure to follo suit once they've been heard."

No surprise for guessing who'd got a cupboard full of the Taiconeroga 45 featured on this comp. However, he should be congratulated for expressing, Homer Simpson-like, the thought running through his head at the time he was writing the sleeve-notes to his latest comp.

Vol. 5 of this benighted series features Glenda Collins' "Thou Shalt Not Steal". Okay, this shows Ritchie Blackmore at his volume-knob waggling, fast-fretting hottest. And it's the best single released in 1965. Full stop. But comped? It's already been rereleased a couple of times to my knowledge on better quality products. Pointless.

The Drippy Hippy's next project? Insiders close to his operation inform me that it's a series of comps called Here Are Some Records I Have From The 1960s Which I Like That Must Be Worth Something. There'll be nine volumes in all. What a wanker!!

Forget what I sed some issues back. THE COMP IS DEAD!!!!!

Myth-Time Inna Music

I find it hard to understand why music's organised in eras. What is this, the early 20th century? Are we really still grokking the matriculation of myth-time? Wood for the trees... vinyl for the plastic... that sort of thing. Why line 'em up and take them one at a time? Letsbeaveinem all at once!!? Set the comp free!!!!

And that's not a genre prejudice directed at the 6Ts crowd, either. These are my deep roots, too. Look, I hunt rock, OK? (Although I like light classical also; it's like orchestrally-oriented psych, but more interesting). Let me set the record straight: the false divisions between rock, pop, reggay, electro, or whatever the latest ones are, also piss me right off.

Throw off your shackles of purchasing torment! (I think we're aksing you to critique and reject the whole notion of "choice" — RH) Unwrap the hard-to-open packaging of taste!! Welcome familiar chords and words like a prodigal sister, not a space alien!!!

To provide total context for my current dismal state of mind (which is entirely the fault of shoddy comp-vendors) let me now deal with the super-crazy tri-action spazzola Unknown Unknowns series, where the value is in the finding and telling, rather than residing mystically somewhere within the mouldy old grooves. Or so I thought.

There used to be some honour in the record collecting game, and at one stage I'd hoped that UU was returning us to that special Golden Age. Of course the comp is not dead, as I previously explained in this organ. It'll never die. It's just a question of how much we can stand up in.

Unknown Unknowns Vol. 1 got me howlin' like a cat in a combine harvester when it was released in 2003. I just missed its first ultra-limited pressing of 150, due to not having the readies, but I caught up with it at last, several months later, courtesy of a certain Brighton record shop, which had one stray copy, delivered totally by mistake.

Where do I start? (Here! Now!! Soon!! Already!!! — RH) The stuff on Vol. 1 was utter dynamite!!! Magnificent ancient mouldy acetates — all crackly and sometimes a little too faint to grasp. Phwoar!! And wot a concept!!!! (Er, that's the part of a church, next to the transept, where they sell people the idea that god will help us — RH) Woah there! These babies were all, as the title suggests, "Unknown" by Unknown!!! Can you get with that?!?!?! Except there was a nice little twist: the last track on Vol 1, side 2 was "Unknown" by The Unknowns — believe it or believe it not!!!

However, Vol. 2, which has just surfaced, is nowhere near as gee-reat as its vinyl ancestor. Sob!! Unlike on it's recently departed relative volume, there's no focus. It's like a nightmare in a salad factory. A bit o' fuzz-bound muscle here, a spartan beat monster there... It's all very well, but I for one need a bit of light and shade for colour and comfort.

I'm envisioning a series of comps called Hubbles, which will basically provide a macroscopic view of the dark musical universe. As the sleeve notes will proudly boast: "Infinitely regressing from the hall of genre mirrors. Exploding, rather than imploding. With open hearts and unchained minds. Let us see the World of Worlds begin!"

Valleys Scoured By Needles

I can't let this ish go by without briefly slagging off Welsh Rare Beat. It seems that one of the lads from the Super Furry Animals has comp'd a load of old Welsh toons released way back when by Sain, Wales's premier Welsh language record label, which is still going today, apparently.

Although there are some lovely melodies therein, I find the Welsh nationalist agenda tiresome. Not to mention that the vast majority of the toons are a load of folky toss. What I found most boring was the lack of Beat numbers, for which the original label and the comp-artist in question should be horse-whipped. Does language-nationalism really have to exile decent music? Look at Van Morrison.

He had to leave Ireland. The only halfway decent rocker in a mire of showbands. Oh, except for The Wheels, the original Afro-Celtic rockers. But I digress.

I'd like to know how such a low-key operation like Sain ran for so long. The compiler fails to inform us how much cash Sain Records got in subsidies from government sources in Westminster. (I'm willing to bet my first hand shandy of the day that they were funded up the wazoo!!) That's probably because he can't admit to himself that the hated English Government had anything to do with keeping the Welsh language alive through education policy and dual-language signage legislation, And it also helped keep the folk music flag flying atop Sain HQ. Funding and subsidies = the death of interesting content.

I've no problem with Welsh culture per se. The poetic tales from "The Black Book of Camarthen" and the transformative, if not exactly pre-Hegelian, bardic practice of Taliesin are constituent parts of the air I breathe. And what of folk? I can get with reconstructionist cultural endeavours every now and then. Jesus! I'm probably the only person in these Atlantic Isles who can construct an sensible argument linking East Anglian Middle English drama of the 14th century (specifically the Cambridgeshire morality epic, "The Castell of Perseveraunce") to reality TV, via Marlowe's "Faustus". And I think I must be the last person in England to pronounce the "g" at the end of "London".

More stuff soon.
Yor Editor

27

25 September 2006

Destroy Cool Shit Before It Destroys You

What a load of mouldy old stuff we've got spinning around on our turntables at the moment. And, wait for it, from the looks of Myspace it seems we're in the throes of another 80s-style garage rock revival, the third this decayed!!!! With all the related toss that goes with it. Dimwit 6Ts couples with not a word of sense between them carbooting for all they're worth. With the splay-leg coffee tables, and the tapping a finger to recent rareities only (not well-known obscurities, if you please), and Tim Warren and his foetid ilk (He's just released their retrospective LP... The Foetid Ilk's, that is!!! — RH) squatting on the whole damn mess. Gawdelpuss!! (Used to have a cat of the very same name!!! — RH)

Like I've said before, Thanes, yes please, Mystreated (or Higher State as is), very nice, thank you. And more of The Sticks, if there's any going!!! But all I can see is a vista crowded with Green sodding Hornets, Mourning Afters, Witchdoktors, and the sorry-arsed like. And I don't know if I've got the strength...

On the bright side, there's always the hope that with greater knowledge than ever before of the toons and style of raw rockin' sounds, we'll get a more tasty, dirtbag-basic approach to torturing the wires — blasting the blackened corpse of taste out of the coffin of professionalism!!! I fear, though, that the focus will, as was certainly the case in the 1980s, be on looking through hair rather than on melody and nice chord-patterns (my ever-present high).

For Link's sake, don't let us fall into the Trap of Cool. What I mean is, I hope bands don't start thinking about dumb spazzola sleazebag grind as part of the 'Great Tradition' to which they must pay homage. Okay, the Top Ten stuff on Nuggets was totally the soundtrack for a generation. But the reanimated product from the vaults, 5c racks, boot-fairs, lofts, attics, served a different purpose, both then and now. It was a way to scratch a mark on the passing culture-stream, dip a toe twice in the same river sort of thing. It was all about hitting and running. Although I'm heavily into revisionism — it was the right thing to do to remind the world, through example, that there were other great groups in the 60s than The Monkees and Jefferson Airplane — I despair of a more inclusive history that serves to incorporate strands of Cool Shit into the Great Tradition of Rock, thereby giving dimwit scenesters, eggheads, and assorted know-it-alls the lowdown on where to get started in the world of media and culture.

I am being timespun back to about 1983, watching the confident middle classes at play with pop culture. We're talking the one their university-educated folks gave em. I got Billy Fury, Little Richard and Duane Eddy. Thanks mum and dad!!! They got The Beatles, William Burroughs, prog, airbrush art, hard and Kraut rock, science and literature. Sound familiar? Well, I can tell you that way back then it mainly added up to Whitesnake, Tolkien and army surplus canvas medic's bags. I was present at the middlebrowing of my generation. And I'm still laughing.

Anyway, with all the versioning of Free Noise, Inner-Space Jaz, Neu-Kraut, psychedelia, Two-Tone, garage punk, or whatever you will, all I can hear is the acculturation — the assimilation, entitling, rite-of passaging, confidence-building — of the comfortable well-to-do, who won't shut about how they've discovered The Cool Shit. Of course, the joke's on them. Because the Cosmick Unzipping they're grokking is actually their ticket to Squaresville, via the University of Rock. Serves them right.

Always with the 'discovering'. Rest assured, all the beat-hot super-dumb fuzz crud was there before 'we' found it and it'll still be there, albeit its DNA and TNT changed a bit by our meddling, after we've passed to glory. When we get records, we must remember we've discovered nothing.

Anyway, who am I kidding? Does anyone care about this stuff any more? Is anyone giving a second, or even a first, thought to what's at stake in replaying all the past all the time? These days, it's all about going forward and moving the agenda on.

General guilt involving everyone taking the blame, even those who consume fuck all and get shafted first has taken over. Even warfare's gone pop. And the wrong of invading lands where people were trying to live their lives in happiness is beyond discussion. It's like the air we breathe.

Two love,
Yore Edyter

28

23 September 2006

Rather Hym Than Mee

Everye now and thenne, over the past few years, my mynde tyrns to rockin' in other spheres outsyde thee plastick grooves spyralling in my lyvyng roome. That's quite enough.

What about all the bands in the movies and on the smaller, less silver, screen? Enduring faves include the unseen but very much heard Electric Banana, doing "Grey Skies" in Tigon Films' excellent Home Counties happening hocum-haze Haunted House Of Horror (1969) and, through a lens, quite darkly, Langston Cove performing "Bank Holiday" almost imperceptibly in the background during "The War Machines", a Dr Who episode in 1966.

Anyway, some American nutter's done what I've been imagining all these years. He's only created lists of groups in the movies! Just sit back, relax, have a think about something and some berk'll do it all for you eventually. That's my way.

Check out the super 60sgaragebands.com for fairly exhausting lists of 1960s rock group TV cameos (1964 .. 1970), rock group feature film cameos (1964 - 1970) and the mysterious-sounding 1960's rock groups' Miscellaneous Appearances (1964 - 1970).

Also, after the Phase IV discovery (meet them at their Myspace page), it looks like there are more fictive funk merchants on the rockin' horizon. Look at a recent Sweet Floral Albion comp and tell me the whole world ain't goin' ROCKHUNTIN'?!?!?!?!

Git some!!!

Unilove me,
Tiye Wsurie

29

30 October 2006

England All Over Again

What's with all the current fuhrer about Yndependente English Musicke at the moment? (C86 is here again!!!!!! Scarper!!!! — RH)

Imagine to my surprise on reading The Guardian the other day only to see that C86 is back on the agenda. More like on the slab as far as I'm concerned. It's pretty miserable to hear about ages past being rechurned, specially when one had a hand in creating them in the first place. Mind you, I've had my hand in quite often over the years. Bit of a hokey cokey merchant with the old hand, me. In out, shake it all about. Etc. Etc. Etc.!!!! And, let's face it, the face of retro has changed out of all recognition since the days when liking old discs was widely thought of as a sign of cultural senility. Yeah, Pricey, Reynolds!! Listen up, you totalitarian pop overlords!!! I remember you oppressing me!!!

Ourselves Alone
C86, Creation And The Celtic Pop Revival In The Atlantic Isles

Here, then, are some reflections about the true context of C86. It seems, on rechecking my bulging archives, that I never published the follow-up piece to Issue 18 I'd intended to write on how Creation Records, in creating a sort of 'retro-activist' musical cell structure in response to the majors' back-cataloguing and the C86 bands' autoethnological revivalism, served as a sort of musical Sinn Fein for independent-minded musicians in the British Isles. And if this is going in the direction I think it is — Celtic Twilight cultural rediscovery and simultaneity goes considerable way to duffing up Empire timeline economics — I still can't be bothered to think of an analogue for James Joyce or the Abbey Theatre. Any suggestions?

See, back in the mid-80s it seemed as though 'we' (those preferring to play guitars and shout) really had got to the stage of thinking of ourselves as being "sons of bastard's ghosts" and had come to view our musical selves as culturally abject in the face of the aggressively 'progressive'-seeming technocracy that had always pushed music capitalism. Musical revivalism and national chauvinism — always sadly a feature of collectorism in rock 'n roll — had contributed to this sense of failure by becoming bogged down in the romanticism of cultural redemption, they merely repeat, uncritically, the discourses of anthropological and cultural domination.

What I'm saying is that Creation Records took on the cultural revival started by the C86 bands and fought the asymmetric retro-wars in a different way, foregrounding its cultural revisionism vis-a-vis exposing the simulateneity, or immanence, of non-popular strands and niches. But it took its heirs — The Kids! — to progressivize their creed by accepting the representation of inauthenticity as authentic critique. And if we are willing to accept that an authentic political critique can emerge from performance — pointing to the kind of 'political education' Franz Fanon talks about — we do so because Creation's ironic recontextualisation and stylistic metacommentary resignifies the experiences of collecting antiquarian sounds as part of a general critique of the effects of record collecting and revivalist discourse on the formation of cultural identities in different places.

It's a case not of valuing self-representation and autoethnographical criticism, but understanding that engagement takes many forms. Perhaps the most important effect of the surprising cultural success of the record collectors' getting across to the gen. pub. the recognition of the simultaneity and pastness of old musics is the emergence of a concept of musical identity freed from the ignominy of primitivism and ethnographic redemption. Collectorism as revisionism is a mode of anti-mimeticism that confronts such a negative vision and puts it under critical pressure. So, yes, I suppose I am saying that collecting records is a form of autoethnographical criticism. And even engagement. Not always, though.

However, the strategies of C86 and Creation, because they lacked the important element of critical self-reflexiveness — like Synge's and Yeats's — forestalled the realization of the problem of authenticity. It is less a matter of finding the appropriate technique for unearthing cultural essences and more about coming to terms with the fact that authenticity is an impossible goal — for the musical revivalist intent on representing 'their' culture as well as for anyone who comes under the sway of (mis) representations claiming to have a purchase on it.

Actually, going back to an earlier point, if revivalist music (your Crypts and Rubbles revisionists, etc.) are JM Synge, and the 'timeless' sounds of berks like The Fuzztones, The Cynics and other eejits stand for WB Yeats, that makes me, Thuh Rockhunter, James Joyce. Not bad, eh?

Thus, from Mod to Garage Punk (itself a term of revivalist rediscovery) to Garage Revival, which is now a thing in itself, reified, to be repeated ad feckin' nauseam. So, some good can come out revivalism. But generally it's not going to change yer life.

Maybe I'll write this properly soon.

For ever and ever. Arseholes.

Tatty bye.

Your editor

30

6 February 2007

Al'ud Dunnit
Al-Andalus, Africa, Sufis, Bards And Blues

Abu l-Hasan, or Ali Ibn Nafi, nicknamed Ziryab, lived from c. 789 to 857 (although he lived according to a different time-rhythm). He was a liberated African slave who first strummed his 'ud at court in Baghdad in the time of Haroun al-Rashid of 1,001 Nights fame. He had to leave Baghdad when he got to hot for them to handle and moved to Córdoba, in Al-Andalus, where he became a bard and boozer. He made himself so popular in Córdoba that people started imitating his manners and fashion sense — even his hairstyles — and he established a school of music that influenced the players and bards of the region for at least two generations after him.

Ziryab mix up the Andalusian music traditions of North Africa and the Middle East and the Arab poetic traditions of qasidah, mwashah and zajal. His distinctive 'ud stylings paved the way for the passionate intermingling of songs, tunes and dances of Persia and Mesopotamia that later, mixed with Gypsy influence, evolved into the famed Spanish flamenco. And it's fair to say that his musical-melodical influence was felt further south in what's now Western Africa.

They say the nickname Ziryab means 'gold finder'. With his emphasis on cultural syntheses of oral traditions, and on the importance of personal style, it's probably fair to say that he was considered something of an alchemist, or finder of gold, in a time of great alchemical explorations. It is significant that the Gold Finder played alchemical guitar left-handed in an area that had already known cultural explorations based on Druidic notions of transmutation and memory.

With the rise of Al-Andalus, the court of Córdoba overtook nearby Seville, with its bishopricк, as the regional cultural centre. Isidore of Seville, originally from Cartagena on the African coast of Iberia, was bishop of Seville from c.600. Isidore was a Christianised Visigoth — a culture that stretched from the Western part of the Frankish lands to Southern Iberia. In his Dark Ages philological masterpiece, Etymologiae, Isidore notes: "[T]he use of letters was invented in order to remember things. For things are fettered by letters in order that they may not escape through forgetfulness [...] letters are signs of things, symbols of words, whose power is so great that without a voice they speak to us the words of the absent; for they introduce words by the eye, not by the ear."

Whether Isidore was replaying his Visigothic roots in recalling the cultural power of transmutation can be fought about elsewhere. Let me just cite this famous passage from The Red Book of Hergest, attributed to Taliesin. Caridwen chases Gwion Bach, who changes shape all the time. Caridwen catches him in a leather bag and throws him in the sea. Gwyddno, the son of Elphin, Taliesin's master, finds the bag with Taliesin inside. The Bards were no strangers to the praxis of transmutation. And it is worthy of note that in another story about Taliesin the place where a cow is sacrificed affords rest to Yssadawr, the deified patriarch (Yssadawr translates as 'consumer', or 'sacrificer'). This link between the Welsh Yssadawr and the Spanish Isidore of Seville is most significant, as it connects two ideas of change employed virtually contemporaneously.

Bardsman's Feast

Everybody got they own thing. And concentrating on transmutation through the collective realisation of personal style is Ziryab's. But where Ziryab, with his freestyle Sufic-bardic roots susses the internal-conversational, even anticlerical, methodology of getting the song across, Isidore brandishes the political tool of secret memory-working (generically, Druidic, in that it was a modus operandi of the Keltoi) but redeploys it to establish the world of letters — truly, the world of the clerics — and thereby written literature, rather than oral culture, as the way forward. Continuity and change. Affectivity and effect. Transmutation of tradition. From druidism to sufism. From Visigothic to Moorish. A local brew.

Nevertheless, both men understand that literal transmutation lies at the heart of cultural production: one thing becomes another, whether it's a melody from one tradition played on the instrument of another, or the understanding that unitary letters invented to aid tribal rhetoric during the wandering and settlement of the various peoples formerly known as Keltoi combine, somewhat surprisingly to spell out — and perhaps, even more surprisingly, effectively atomize — the Word of God.

By now you'll have guessed that I'm venturing into the last bastion of the music journalistic scoundrel: the origin of the blues. Well, make no mistake, I'm not going to get into an argument about which is the more authentic, oral or written culture. That's not important right now. Neither is it a matter of assigning a particular location of origin for something that is and was multivalent and multifarious. So what if I said Al-Andalus was the home of the blues?

If we accept as gospel what some American Muslims have noticed about the similarity of, say, the cadences of work songs like "Levee Camp Holler" and the call to prayer, then, yes, it's easy to say that the blues is the cultural heritage of Muslim slaves, whether sung or played on the guitar. However, although historical revisionism is history, cultural separatism is just stupid. Lest us not forget that the search for the pure sound that defines a people, were it used in Al-Andalus 1,100 years or so ago, would have ruled out the mix-up inventions of Muslim slaves like Ziryab, whose famous 'ud styling changed the perception of music even more in its remembrance than within earshot.

On a slight diversion, according to various newspapers reports rehashing promotional information from guitar retailers, guitar sales are going through the roof. More people are buying them than ever before, and it's possible that more are being bought now than during the First Beat Boom.

Of course, only the tiniest percentage of guitars sold will ever be used to play a tune all the way through. Most of these instruments will be chucked in a cupboard by the kids they've been presented to and forgotten once they've understood that practising is tedious and takes up time that could be better spent quaffing bottles of sweetened alcohol and taking pictures of their mates with camera phones and showing them immediately how they look.

Six-string mediocrity onslaught? Don't blame Ziryab, he didn't invent the blues.

I'm gone.
Your Editor

Edit: Recent genetic research shows similarities between Y chromosome types found in Somalia, Oman, Egypt and Iraq and, albeit at low frequencies, in France, Spain, Portugal and Britain. So the historical links between the middle east and Iberia and between Iberia and Britain become more tenable.

31

29 January 2007

Versions And Voices
English Language Fashion From Frank Spencer To Jamie T

One of the best things about living in England is the pace of change in speech fashions. Other countries move glacially slow. I'm thinking France, USA, and loads of other places I haven't really thought enough about. But here in England, we got it going on. Half the time, no one knows what the other half is saying. I was born in Cambridge and used to work in bookshops there, so I'm well aware that the elites have always had their special way of excluding others, even members of the same group, through language. And that works every which way, through every hierarchy that you can think of. Language is a generator of individualism like no other. For even later-capitalist marketing exploits community niches.

Anyway, what I'm talking about today is language and pop music. Ever since I switched my music antenna back on a few years ago, after not being bothered with the present for most of the 1980s and 1990s, I noticed the Frank Spencer effect creeping in. From "Oo-bla-dee" to Jamie T.

It was Elvis Presley, mumbling like he was singing for himself in a room alone. Or Jimmy Reed, who couldn't help having a drink before recording his tunes, thereby commiting to vinyl his 'mushmouth' singing style. Or Jimmie Rodgers, shouting high above the noise of the bar, loud enough to be heard and slurring due to spotted lungs. Depending on who you believe. Take your pick. Black or white. If you feel you have to choose who was first. We're talking about language fashions, picked up and projected all over the place all at once. Come to think of it, Flanagan and Allen did their bit for down-home mush-mouth renditions. They're the original version of the pub singer type that everyone's been mocking since Billy Connolly gently did it a few years back. Only there's been no pub singers for many, many years. And karaoke is not the same thing at all.

Language fashion is not a new thing in England. Consider Charles Mackay's Memoirs of Extraordinary Popular Delusions and the Madness of Crowds (1852), which includes a chapter called "Popular Follies of Great Cities", in which he ruminates on the peculiarities of fashionable phraseology, including the fleeting use of the portmanteau word, "QUOZ", or the question "Who are you?" that still lingers on football terraces to this day. Think about all the British movies made from the 1930s to early 1960s. Chock full of Americanisms, from Noir to Beat, filtered through feature films, Jazz and Blues. I'm well aware that E17 were not the the first English people to try and exoticise or de-Anglicise their speaking voices. Although their singing voices were quite angelic, all things considered. Anyway, it was Tim Westwood, the big wanker, who did it first for this new generation. And the "Big Dog" — a homage to the ghostly dog, Black Shuck, a legend in his former East Anglian 'hood? — himself has gone through several linguistic refits since trying New York on for size back in the 1980s. At the moment, he's reprezentin his endz the only way he knows how, by trying out South London Jam-African.

Now I think of it, it was Ray Gange in The Clash's movie vehicle Rude Boy (1980) who I first noticed doing the back-of-the-throat, fly-catching mushmouth South London. He definitely put a "w" in "boy", as my memory recalls. See? This is the trouble with origins, they just keep going back. And before you know it, they're totally outta sight! That's why I generally stick to my extreme presentist and poetic take on Marxiana. With a shang-a-lang-a-dooby-wah! Prole-Voola!

Right, back in the world with Jamie T, well aware that he's doing different in creating a dolce stil novo, like Dante did in La Divina Commedia. We get a hint of what's involved in this social intervention from the use of a schoolmaster's voice admonishing some of his charges for the "blue-blooded murder of the English tongue" in a received pronounciation sample in "Sheila", available on the lad's own corner of MurdochSpace. Hate to drag the dead into the proceedings, but there's a shitload of Joe Strummer in Jamie T's delivery. Not sure whether that's just the thing with broken toothed singers, but the former's phrasing's got shades of the latter's. Anyway, I shouldn't care to share a lift with either of them. In the case of Strummer, I wouldn't have done so even before he'd died. I reckon with enough episodes of Some Mothers Do 'Ave 'Em under his belt, Jamie T would be singing a different tune. Maybe even "Hello My Darlings", as versioned by Charlie Drake.

What's all this about Frank Spencer? Well, dat's the ting with Anglicised versions of patois, without wishing to come all over David Starkey, it makes the speaker sound like Frank Spencer.

Down here in Brighton, there's not much sign of it in the Indie community, which is pretty solidly Americanist. But being in the company of students, albeit at a distance, it's quite obviously a massive influence on well-heeled youngsters. The Spencerisation Project is huge. The middle classes, the crossest of all the classes, love being able to assert themselves even more thoroughly. And they must percieve that the emphatic nature of Jamaicaphonics gives them an edge in social situations.

Where was I? Oh yeah, the first time I encountered Spencerisation, I laughed out loud on recognising it. It was transported back to the late 1970s, when every rotten ITV impressionist did Frank Spencer. Especially Lenny Henry, the big tosser, who was the last impressionist ever to get paid for doing it!

Me? I'm stickin to my chops, daddy-o! They do right by me. Everyone knows what I grok. Dig? Like, it's now! I ain't no Time Travel Agent!

Pull my finger.
Your Editor

32

28 February 2007

Generic Psych And The Realism Of Sublime Repetition

For the past two months, I've been listening to just one cassette tape every day. And I plan to listen to it until I get bored with a single song. As yet, due to the subject knowledge and aural astuteness of the compiler, there's no sign of boredom setting in. But that's fine.

The cassette in question was made by a friend a dozen or so years ago and is skilfully compiled from tracks avaiable on various comps in the mid-1990s. The whole of Side A is taken up with Incredible Film Show Stories, Vol. 1 (Dig the Fuzz, 1995), containing some of my all-time favourite all-time favourites. Side B comprises a swim through the backwaters of psych, from 'A' to beat. If you get me.

Here's the track listing of an unlabelled Frankenstein's Comp that I have come affectionately to call "Christian's Generic Psych".

Side A

1. The Ricketts, "Action Painting", 1969 original release (Germany)
2. The Primitives, "Oh Mary", 1966 original release (Oxford)
3. Liverpool Five, "Gotta Get A Move On", 1967 original release (London)
4. The Barrier Dawn Breaks Through 4 1968 original release (Fulham)
5. Unknown, "Strange World", 1967 original release
6. Phase 4, "Listen To The Blues", 1966 original release (Southampton)
7. The Belfast Gypsies, "The Gorilla", original release (Belfast)
8. Arthur Brown & The Diamonds, "You Don't Know" 1965 original release (England)
9. The Glass Sun, "Silence Of The Morning" original release (Ypsilanti, Michigain)
10. The Maze, "I'm So Glad", 1967 original release (Slough)
11. The Limit, "Happy Life" 5/1969 original release (Adelaide)
12. The You-Know-Who Group!!, "(Roses Are Red) My Love", 1964 original release (Liverpool)
13. Unknown, "Red And Green Talking Machine", 1967 original release
14. The Purple Barrier, "Shapes And Sounds", 1968 original release (Fulham)
15. Anthony Dare's Progress, "Devil" 1966 unreleased (Nottingham)
16. Information, "Face To The Sun", 1970 original release (UK)
17. Blues & Roots, "Blue Root" (mis-titled as "Getting It"), 1964 unreleased (Nottingham)

Side B

1. Pink Floyd, "Candy and Currant Bun"

2. Unknown to me. [Chorus: "It's been a long time coming, but you've got to hold on/It's been a long time coming, but the past has gone"]

3. Fire, "Flies Like a Bird"

4. Sharon Tandy & Fleur De Lys, "Hold On"

5. The Buzz, "You're Holding Me Down"

6. The Fairytale, "Listen To Mary Cry"

7. The Poets, "Wooden Spoon"

8. The Fairytale, "Guess I Was Dreaming"

9. Les Sauterelles, "Dream Machine"

10 The Attack, "Lady Orange Peel"

11. The Poets, "In Your Tower"

12. Kaleidoscope, "Dive into yesterday"

13. Unknown, "Can't Stop The Want I Got For You Babe"

14. The Exiles, "Love In The Making"

15. The Birds, "How Can it Be?"

16. Ipsissimus, "Hold On"

Tracks 6 to 11 from *Adventures in the Mist, Rubbles 11*, 1988, Bam Caruso Records. Tracks 13 & 14 from *Hen's Teeth Volume 2: Blocked! Rare Beat & Psychedelia.* Other tracks from like elsewhere

Beat Music Becomes Real

I'll be writing about these tunes in the next few issues. What they mean to me, in and out of context, and how my response to them changes over time. Everything is fine. Thee Rockhunter would like to hear people's thoughts on these tunes and on listening obsessively to particular songs and styles. All will be well. Your Editor is merely a ganglion in the marginalia.

The main reason for doing this, other than loving the sound of my own typing, is a perpetual annoyance with reviews of this sorta stuff that rarely, if ever, venture far from the subjects set down in lore by the Tim Warren and the fraternity lads of Snooty Wow Yappa. Either that, or the reviewers are likening the tunes they're yakking on about to others that they've heard. What about the work at hand? Do these songs only exist to bulk out their collections of similar? So that's what this is all about. I welcome corrections, improvements, general comments and even random thoughts generated by the tunes or my endangered pedestrian prose.

I don't feel trapped. Help me. I do not think I need help to solve The Mystery of Generic Psych and the Realism of Sublime Repetition. Can we really change our reality simply by working together? How can making a compilation of our thoughts and feelings possibly make a difference? It would be nice to go somewhere else. But can we really leave our lives of sublime repetition and escape?

In any event, I'd be grateful for help identifying the one totally unknown and the known unknown on Side B.

Two love
Your Editor

33

6 March 2007

Generic Psych and the Realism of Sublime Repetition, II

Christian's Generic Psych: Side A, Track 1: "Action Painting" by The Ricketts

Some have called The Ricketts' 1969 version of this tune a freakbeat classic, and others have simply referred to it as a tedious psychey workout by that was too late to fit its niche. However the vinyl cookie crumbles — and all records must fall to dust, leaving only reverberations in the aether — it's a perfect, understated example of the instro-mentality . That is, take a tune you know and play it under your own title to people who haven't cottoned on to what it is. Bingo! You've got an extra number on your set list for very little effort expended. And it's always best to do as The Ricketts do: wait a few years till the prototype's been consigned to the rock 'n' pop oubliette. Oh, and play it in another country where the original's hard to find. And give it a more uptadate title.

From chord 1, The Ricketts launch themselves with the discipline of showtime troupers into a controlled-feedback creep through a much-loved live number. It takes its time, like only a 1960s instrumental B-side can. It's all about the players and the playing. It's not the most immediate choice for a first track, but perhaps Dig the Fuzz was going for a "live set" feel, putting an opening number first.

The form and ideology of the rock instrumental is a much-understudied area of research. For one thing, instrumentals defy rock 'critics' to come up with readable copy. That's why they're rarely, if ever, written about at length. Rock writers only know enough about music to comment on the clothes and overt musical references. They know nothing else.

To put the toon in con-text, it's a total rip of The Rolling Stones' "2120 South Michigan Avenue", recorded by Wanker, Phelche and the lads in a 1964 session at Chess Studios, one of the greatest beating hearts of black culture in the whole world. Bo Diddley, Howlin' Wolf, Willie Dixon and Chuck Berry had recorded there a couple of times before the Stones flew over, just to check it was okay for The Fauntleroys (as the Chess regulars lovingly called 'em) to use. But it seems the Stones were happy with the facilities and liked the place enough to name a whole song after the studio's Chicago address.

The Stones' version of this tune was first released in the UK on "Five by Five" EP in the summer of 1964, then in the US on the "12x5" LP that winter. A version was also recorded for a BBC Radio session in 1964.

As Band 1, Side 1 of the Generic Psych tape, "Action Painting" is the signal for the volutionary cycle of Generic Psych to commence afresh. Despite the title, this is less pop art than an industrial product. When The Chantays ditched the title of their instrumental number, "Liberty's Whip" and renamed it "Pipeline" they leapt from rockin' dance-band stylings to Surf and thence the record charts. The Ricketts, by way of contrast, did something far more interesting with their retitled instrumental number, which self-consciously reanimates a moribund popular conception of the pop art process. Like The Timelords in the late 1980s[1], The Ricketts redirected a discarded discourse through the medium of the rock, or pop, instrumental. Like Naughty Cauty and his glowering pal after them, The Ricketts took it upon themselves to act as cultural divines and comment, from that lofty position,

[1] The Timelords' "Doctorin' the Tardis" (1988) was that rarest of pop beasts, the instrumental with words.

silently, in music, on the aching void (Ooh, me Emmas RH) that had apparently opened in pop culture after London had ceased, in the popular imagination, to move in a pendular fashion. It's a bit like if the Pet Shop Boys did an instrumental called "Conceptual Death Camp". Or something far funnier, if you'd prefer it. Don't get me wrong, the 1960s got a whole load more industrial than The Ricketts. But theirs ain't no meaned achievement for a tune with no words.

The Ricketts are not to be confused with (Jimmy &) The Rackets ("Skinny Minnie"/"O Mona", Elite, 1964/65, and other releases), an English band who rocked in exile in Deutschland, playing for US servicemen and on package tours with The Beatles and The Kinks.

All the best
Your Editor

34

10 March 2007

Violent Inversions And Gender Role Reinforcement

The videos for Lily Allen's "Smile" and Avril Lavigne's "Girlfriend" fulfil similar functions in marketing the idea of gender-centered empowerment. On the face of it, with totally different agendas, these two women allow themselves to be used in a tedious reworking of The Battle of the Sexes. Allen's on-screen persona hires some street-punks to beat up her ex-boyfriend and trash his flat. Meanwhile, elsewhere in the rockin' multiverse, Lavigne's goth-punk character does violence to a rather anodyne version of herself.

Allen's video perpetuates the stereotype of the woman scorned, who feels she has a licence to commit violence. It's a version of the evergreen "I cut his clothes to ribbons because he left me for another woman" narrative. There's a similar ad running on telly at the moment, where women are portrayed committing criminal damage to their partners' property for apparently disrespecting their own. Anyway, your woman, Allen, hangs around, with butter unmelted in her gob, sticking her tongue out coquettishly and rolling her rich eyeballs, paying a bunch of toughs in cool hard cash for duffing up the unfortunate fellow who messed with poor li'l Lily's persona's head.

Lavigne's character is a more ironic take on the high school relationships scene. The goth-punk girl doesn't really wanna be with the jerk-off jock she's eyeballing, but she wouldn't mind a go on him anyway. However, for some reason, Lavigne insists on coyly re-reunning the girlfriend/boyfriend concept for the 100000000000000th time — not being able to admit in song that she wants to have sex with the fellow. And for this reason, the other woman, also played by Lavigne, gets it in various high school-related ways.

How I hate inverted gender taxonomies.

Charlie Brooker Must Try To Become Less Ubiquitous

This week, as part of his increasing exposure in print and on telly, Brooker produced an article in The Guardian about why he hates his new mobile phone. I can't be bothered to explain why I hate newspaper columnists who produce this sort of toss, so you'll just have to imagine it.

New Comps News

I seem to have missed An Experiment With Tyme, Vol. I (Swozzle, 2006) when it was first out, but that's not that unusual. I haven't got the cash these days to spend on discs. Most of my spare coppers go on eatin' treats from the deli over the road. I love a nice rye loaf, with a bit of quality serano and a tub of mixed olives. And as far as music goes, as I'm currently documenting in other posts, my listening needs on a daily basis, at least to and from work, are entirely satisfied by Christian's Generic Psych cassette. Interestingly, I bumped into Simon this afternoon and Christian had done him a tape around the same time, which seems to contain exactly the same tracks! How many more are out there? And what can it all mean?

Anyway, back to the matter in hand. I was up in London yesterday and rounded a very nice afternoon off with some fine, competitively priced Pakistani cuisine at the Lahore Kebab House on Umberston Road, about 10 minutes from Aldgate East tube. The lamb chops for starters were fantastic, but were narrowly pipped to the post by the chicken and spinach main course. I was stuffed to the gunnels for under a tenner! You'll have to take your own booze, though, as they don't have a licence. The mango lassi looked good, though if you're contemplating the benefits of temperance.

Where was I? Oh yeah, this wretched comp I stumped up just under a tenner for. Was it worth it? Are they ever? Band 4, Side 2 is my top tip on this waxing. Why, it's "Footpath to Lavender St." by Christopher Eager, the original 45 of which is, in my world, as rare as magic rocking horse shit. The bi-side of "Your Carriage Awaits", comped a few years back, this intriguing Future-period Seeds-style number is a rather pleasant opener. From the other face of the disc I was expecting harpsichords, paeans to Morgantown and so forth. But there's an almost Brechtian use here of what I term the Michigan Muffle - that is, recording an overamped guitar at full volume with minimal compression and damping it in the mix a bit. I'm thinking The Glass Sun's "In the Silence of the Morning", if you need a comparison. With this technique, there's a distancing of the sound, thru its imperfect reproduction, that renders it a highly visible, almost tangible, presence.

Who knows who produced this waxy earacher, but it's certainly not the same engineer that did the radio side. Eager sounds a little uncomfortable with the result. It's almost as if he's written the words to fit a different version. This 1967 song appears to be about a young man's faltering steps through a London of the imagination, from theatreland to drinking clubs, significantly via Picadilly. The couplet, "Music is my trade / I feel my vision fade / Singing's not for free / I get it on HP", is the key to the whole number. Given the name of the tune, it's pretty fair to suggest that "trade" is actually the Palare slang for a person one has sex with, and "HP" in that case would stand not for "hire purchase", but "homy palome", or homosexual man. Whether he knows it or not — and I suspect that he did, because the songwriter's name, C. Ede, has the same initials as its singer's — Christopher Eager was singing about the road to self-realisation of a gay man in London's entertainment business. I wonder what happened to him after this single went down the toilet? So to speak.

Despite this comp's excellent title, the rest of the tunes on are much less intriguing than the Eager number. This whole comp business is like a nightmare in a salad factory. Of the other tracks, my faves so far are Poor Wight's "Upside-Down Heart", which is a great stomper straight outta 1968. And I actually enjoyed Still Water's version of "Eight Miles High". Get me? ENJOYED!!! Perhaps it's because they do it cool, like 4tathafloor. Fuzz monsters are all very well, but baby I need a bit of light and shade. You understand me? For colour and comfort. Dig?

In Future Issues

- 45 Me: a definitive guide to the best bands for singles As and Bs? (Gotta be a toss-up between The Kinks, The Troggs and The Buzzcocks. (I'd pay a not inconsiderable sum to see Shelley and Presley — hem, hem — "compete" in that manner — RH)
- Post-Punk: contriving controversy: what is it, exactly? In fact, what are they talking about? (It's the old game of "Who d'you like best?" Wotta crock! Vote now!!! Tommy Steele or PiL!! — RH)
- A Brief History of the Black and White Panthers and the Great Might-Have-Been of British Rock 'n' Roll Radicalism. But all we got was the great divide between asceticism and excess, and we were lucky to wind up with Tom Robinson and Billy Bragg, God help us.
- Rain Effects in Rock 'n' Roll, Part II
- No Retro: Why the Past is Already Here
- The Medway Drummers: the unique, localised sound/ style that changed the course of backstoried re-enactment rock 'n' roll.
- And so much more....
- Hey! This ain't Pismo Beach!

That's all folks!
Hugs.
Your Editor

35

26 March 2007

Generic Psych and the Realism of Sublime Repetition, III

Christian's Generic Psych Tape: Side A, Track 2: "Oh Mary", The Primitives

It's impossible to overstate the importance of The Seeds' influence on beat music in the British Isles in the second half of the 1960s. My pal Dave was turned on to their sound by his friend in 1967 and they used to play a couple of Seeds numbers live in their Woodingdean-based band. "Oh Mary" by The Primitives, released in 1966 on an EP with "I Don't Feel Myself" on the face-up and "Mr. Heartache" b/w "Tears In My Eyes" on the flip (Vogue INT 18093), combines the solid A/G versifying of The Seeds with a trebly, yet still bone-shaking, near-negation of the power chord lifted from anything from The Who up to 1966, or The Kinks to 1965. The off-kilter effect of this non-power chord provides a poignant counterpoint to the linear thrust of the song's arrangement.

I first heard The Primitives in 1985 courtesy of the inclusion of their life-affirming, ranting rave, "Yeeeeeeah!", on Pebbles, Volume 18: The Continent Lashes Back, European Garage Rock, Part 2. This 1967 Italian single is a more trippy number, which had led me to figure the band as a bunch of stoners giving up a futile, blissed-out version of the late-60s counter-culture "message". But they're right on the money with "Oh Mary", a bass-thumping club classic before its time.

The Primitives were from these Isles, but left them behind in the mid-60s to work in mainland Europe, mainly Italy, I think. That well-trod path had been trampled down by many before them, including The Beatles, who rocked it most nights, mornings, afternoons and evenings in down-town Hamburg. This exodus of talent has for too long been regarded as a sign of a band's uselessness. In fact, it's a reflection of their ability to keep audiences interested all over the place and, therefore, a marker of how good they are at entertaining.

Contrary to the expectations of those who've seen their fair share of John Waters movies, "Oh Mary" is not a camp address to another man in the feminine diminutive, although it suggests the gaiety of a party-goer, nor is it a paean to some renamed Apollonian deity after the Greek fashion, although it is clearly a song of praise and joy. Mal Ryder of The Primitives, if indeed it is he, offers his Mary a sweet plea: "I been waiting all my life, for someone like you / But now you've turned away from me now / You say that I won't do…"

I can't make out whether it's the recording of the instrumentation that makes this a thin song. It could be the natural reverb of the room it was recorded in that interpellates the slight interference, or phasing, characteristic of recordings made with a cheap microphone. Or, having thought about it for a couple more minutes, the thin sound could be a result of the compiler mastering from an extant copy of the record, maybe even from a test pressing. That would account for the rather distant quality of the recording. But suffice it to say it's fat in all the right places.

See ya,
Your Editor

36

31 August 2007

Hauntiquarianism
Divergency, Amateurism, Mundaneity And Laughter

I'm suppressing Rockhunter and transforming it into Rockhaunter on 31 August 2007. Having thought about the interplay between antiquarianism, popular music, fictional histories and tradition for a long time, that was the day I realised and professed that I was a hauntiquary — and probably had been all along! On discovering this truth, I immediately invented the term "hauntiquarianism" to describe my endeavours.

Hauntiquarianism is envisaged as a jolly response to, and furtherance of, current discussions of hauntology, which seem, due to the small number of participants, to be reaching a consensus on music, film, topography and local history. Rockhaunting is all about arguing about the provenance and depositioning of antiquarian sound and vision till reason laughs.

Coming soon: Rockhaunter No. 1, Halloween Hauntology Special

Rockhaunter: Your No. 1 Site For Hauntiquarianism Not Hauntology!

I've been thinking about the interplay between antiquarianism, popular music, fictional history and tradition. That may lead me to do something on hauntology, because it seems that my arc of fire has touched that of others thinking about where popular music's been and gone — and my arc's zxzxzxzxzx'd significantly.

In fact, I'll do it now. I've long since made a conscious effort not to collect music but to describe my relationship with its creation. Ergo, I'm a Rockhaunter. I'm going to rename my what I do as "Hauntiquarianism". Which makes me a hauntiquarian or hauntiquary. That's the first time those words have ever been written, etymology fans, though others including me have probably thought them.

Since Rockhaunting's all about antiquarian sounds and arguing about their provenance till reason laughs, I'm claiming what's rightly mine. Since history belongs in the fiction section, along with the other realisms, I'm the man who cometh in this hour. Since the death of pop music is what I'm all about, it's only right that I stand up and be ignored in the great debate that's currently shaking our universities apart with frequencies often beyond the range of normal men.

I and I am a hauntiquarian, although I didn't know it until recently. The simultaneity of experience is what I'm about, in all spaces and dimensions. (But don't give up your own views and actions, thinking others will take up the slack.) I'm seeking a way beyond antiquarianism, while retaining the vital amateurism of independent research, and beyond Hauntology, which sounds fine but is a reinvention of historicism with weird contingencies replacing science.

Why Hauntiquarianism?

The idea of hauntology, as inherited from Jacques Derrida (who invented the word as a spectral pun on 'ontology') and reworked by contemporary intellectuals, is concerned with the knowability of cultural artefacts and trends that are affirmed by the continual reappearance and presence and/or apparent absence of archetypes; it seeks to distinguish between the paucity of fixed, historical meanings and the fecundity of non-chronological ones. Popular music, for example, is generally thought to be knowable because of the reiteration of a fixed series of historical points back into the past. However, the reappearance, presence and/or absence of historical figures — the constant historicist shifting of focus between past and present — that comprises the formation of the idea of popular music means that it is becoming more present, solid and knowable in time and fainter, less knowable and less historical as its non-presence is appreciated.

It seems to me that what the hauntology writers are doing is regarding sublime landscapes in the manner of a sketchy aristo on the Grand Tour. In regarding the play of cultural and topographical shadows in gauzy spaces that overlap fleetingly, they neglect to imagine that their choice of active contemplation came from somewhere and imply that space is mostly devoid of conscious affective actions. In fact, it's worse than that, because they are regarding sublime landscapes as forgotten or uncomplete ideological statements, as they wander, recreating and finishing them — even if they are completed thoughts in space/time — in their own image with synthesizers and critical theory.

In any non-event, people make places. There's no emptiness, no silence. Let's let the voices through. But should we use ventriloquism or listen to the sibilant hiss and pop of the archive flowing? Or would you prefer to regard the lips of a hauntologist moving in time to a post-punk soundtrack — singing along to the adverts of the gone future?

I think the hauntologists might find it helpful to read my ongoing reflections on iteration in my occasional series on discovering the sublimity of repetition through repeated listening to generic psych, in which I analyse the effect on me of listening only to a C90 cassette recording of psychedelic pop tunes from the late-1960s over a period of three months while commuting.

Do You Like Soil Music?

Landscapes are subjective. It's that interpretative quality that allows their narration to be taken as representing something wider or something else entirely. The Specials' single, "Ghost Town", for example, was taken by young people, who walk through places at night, as an anthem about their city, town, village or hamlet. You can get that effect in pop music, because not having to take it so seriously, people feel free to insert their own continuation narratives in the spaces left by the song writers and music arrangers. But writers in the throes of ecstacy, having found a place that fits or fixes an idea perfectly, should always be aware that the affectivity of their sensitive subjectivity may not leave as light a mark as they'd hoped, even if they bear in mind the interlinked matters of class, place and money.

That's the big problem with W G Sebald. In "Rings of Saturn", he depopulates the bit of Suffolk he writes about so as to find space in which to locate his intellect and grief. Some have called this manoeuvre spectral geography. I call it a flaming cheek. Can you imagine imagining empty landscapes in a period just after ethnic cleansing elsewhere in Europe?

Q: What's A Burial Urn?
A: About £150 A Week

Sebald was partly inspired by Sir Thomas Browne, who like many antiquarians thought a lot about the irony of corporeal impermanence being represented in long-lived material culture, whether stone — mememto mori or statuary — or the written word. However, Browne wrote Hydriotaphia, Urn Burial, or a Discourse of the Sepulchral Urns lately found in Norfolk as a tribute to the gone generations who'd thought enough of their dead kin, whether sublimely or materially, to find a place for them after death. They had not vanished into ideological aether, although they were assimilated into collective representation through ritual. They were known individuals, the knowing of whom left the underground as peopled as the ground above.

Around the time Sebald was writing "Rings of Saturn", someone I knew well was dying in a Suffolk coastal town. His ashes were scattered on a bit of water near Oulton Broad. There was nothing spectral either about his dying or the simultaneity of his lived experience (felt now in memory) and his not being there any more.

Maybe our two spectral geographies clash, mine and Sebald's. Maybe I'm fighting a dead man's dream of future contentment. Maybe I can see his lips moving. Either way, I'll get the last word in. If you want to canvas his opinion, read the books he's still writing. Or ask his shade, still haunting the Lowestoft region as he haunted it in life.

Antiquarianism vs. Realism?

I've as much a problem with the hauntologists regarding sublime scenes as I had with Julian Cope doing something similar in his Modern Antiquarian phase: reciting poetry in the wind whistling between standing stones. Are we to just regard these things as the remains of the good that's gone? I sympathise with Cope's implication that the down-playing of antiquarianism by historians, writers of fiction that is, means that the former practice has a place and purpose that history — fictive filing — can't even aspire to. But the antiquaries were not druid descendants, as Cope imagined them. These were independent intellectuals who wanted everyone to know what they'd found and what they thought about it, unlike the druids who were the epitome of unfreedom, a ruling body of secretive professionals denying affective knowledge and thought to the rest of their people.

In practice, like all amateurs, the antiquarians were dull, careful, maverick, wrong, inspired; these were people with diverse and often irreconcilable dreams and interests. Above all, though, they took it upon themselves to go out and have a look for themselves, ask others what they'd seen, and to collect and sometimes to write about the material cultures of the past and present. In doing so, often within territories they'd earmarked for themselves around where they lived, but also in larger territories, and in attempting to understand the fragmentary and fleeting nature of those material cultures, they came to appreciate the relatively low limits of realism and representation as science — which was were history as a practice and discipline started — and the relatively high limits of locality as a unit of human experience and understanding.

Hunting vs. Haunting. Hauntiquarianism vs. Hauntology

If we're talking about making something beyond realism and history, then that's a fine thing. Most of human life is beyond the scope of the real and history. History is the dead thing we worry about not having. It's been that way since its state-sponsored beginnings. Reality is what we create in daydreams. It's always been that way. But to reinvent death and daydreams by circumlocution is a poor waste. Let's have a waste we can love.

How I Became a Hauntiquarian

It seems I've been a hauntiquarian all along. It's only recently I knew what it meant, due to hauntologists starting to describe what I do, but using the wrong word. We're just coming to understand the low limits of realism and the extent of the convergency between history, fiction, realism and the sublime. In a time of convergency, I'm all for divergency. In a hauntological milieu, I'm a hauntiquarian.

Your Editor,
Thee Rockhaunter

Rockhaunter

No. 1
September 2007

First issued on 2-sided A4 around Brighton, Thursday 6 September to Saturday 8 September.

As befits a wraith, this publication shall remain etheric, the better to haunt the visible world.

Rockhaunter

No. 2
Undated

Boredom Or Sublime Repetition

I guess I've tested, nearly to my own destruction, the realism of genre music. I'm glad I'm telling somebody about this.

And so we continue the saga of Christian's Generic Psych, with the rest of Side A, followed swiftly by Side B.

3. Liverpool Five, "Gotta Get a Move On" (TK, 1967)

Like they say, it's a hurry-up paean to getting cracking. No messing about. A fiery rhythm gtr and a pounding bass do the business amid waling b/voc.

4. The Barrier, "Dawn Breaks Through" (Eyemark, 1968)

This either is or is not a song about watching the sun come up over Fulham. There's at least a couple of levels of reality overlapping here. But it could just as easily be an imaginary seasidescape: "Ships are sailing, birds are flying / Lighthouse blinking, sun shines down / The roofs are crooked, waifs are all around me. It's about how ancient the present can be when you think about it.

The fact about The Barrier that I know is that Alan Brooks was later in Punchin' Judy.

Lead gtr
Strident bass
Drums
Vocal

5. Unknown, "Flies on the Screen" (or "Strange World") (Unreleased, 1967)

Deep lyrics. I wish I'd written this.

6. Phase 4, "Listen To The Blues" (Fab, 1966)

This is the only genuine pop number on Christian's tape. The singer is a bit flat, though, which is probably how it got into the collectable (i.e. discarded) bracket. Why wasn't this more popular and thus well known today? Was quality control better in the past? Well, it's a consideration. Maybe his trousers weren't as good as the other lads'. Or perhaps he'd a wall eye or not enough charisma.

7. The Belfast Gypsies, "The Gorilla" (Vogue, No Date)

It's a go-go instrumental. Stop.

8. Arthur Brown & The Diamonds, "You Don't Know" (Lyntone, 1965)

Rock solid beat. Showboat soulfulness, but more Screaming Jay Hawkins than James Carr. Sung in a self-consciously 'Negro' way in parts — the Chris Farlowe effect — like he's listened to Blues records properly, plus "Porgy and Bess" and "The Black and White Minstrel Show".

The 'he' in question? None other than Arthur Brown, the man who sang "Fire". He's currently living in East Sussex. He occasionally reprises his "Fire" act in Brighton and elsewhere. He is very tall and whenever I've seen him wandering round town, he's seemed quite contented.

This is a sinister song. There's a sense of a stalker summing up his passionate non-relationship. When Brown croons, "You don't know — you can't know!", it's almost as if he's got something on the object of his unrequited attentions and has taken umbrage at the suggestion, which he's just conjured up out of nowhere, that they may actually come to divine his love intentions. In short, this is not a serenade but a hymn to narcissism. The teenage Brown narrates in a voice thick with stagey passion, almost strangled, like Kenneth Connor, by imaginary bridled lust. I've used that phrase many times before, but it's a good one and should be said more often.

9. The Glass Sun, "Silence Of The Morning" (Sound Patterns, No Date)

This band's name encapsulates a whole world of late-urban shamanistic discovery. It refers first to a light blub, then to a stoned appreciation of the possibility of sitting in the sun looking out from the inside. I've read that they came from Michigan, but I don't know for certain. Actually, there's not much I do know for certain. Anyway, you don't want to hear me running on.

"Silence of the Morning" is heavier than Robbie Coltrane on Boxing Day. The singer has abandoned vocal intensity in favour of volume, recalling David Peel's voicings during his King of Punk period. In the same way, presumably, that Jeezuz the Nazarene was Rex Iudi. The gtr performs a massive, mighty fuzz riff that's so heavy it's structural. This is one of – hang on, probably the only — extended freakout numbers I've ever actually enjoyed. Although I'm still partial, every now and then, to a bit of "Into the Maelstrom", by Radio Birdman. That sort of caper. But I wouldn't want it every morning, if you know what I mean.

Suffice it to write that the kids are nowhere near so silent in their loudness these days. The Glass Sun sings about the end of unconscious teenage and the beginning of their conscious minds and poetry: they're shouting about the beauty of silence.

10. The Maze, "I'm So Glad" (Vogue International, 1967)

It's a dead rip-off of Cream! Exactly the same arrangement. Not a hint of Skip James left in the poor old tune. Only the descending trebly ld. gtr. owes anything to James's country blues stlyings.

There's a condenser mic sound on the vocals. Again, as with The Ricketts's "Action Painting", I'm left wondering whether this is due to recovering the sound from a record or acetate, or whether it's down to the recording. It's even possible that the vocals were recorded through an amp mic'd up in the studio.

Ian Gillan, later of Deep Purple and, even later, the rather sad Oafmeister of the Sounds weekly music paper's trend they called NWOBHM (That's New Wave of British Heavy Metal, for the benefit of the young reader— RH), sang on this recording. Amen.

11. The Limit, "Happy Life"(RCA, 1969)

Starts up with a couple of power chords straight out of the book written by The Game, circa "It's Shocking What They Call Me"., after which the sound engineer reigns the chaps back in and they carry on with a verse-heavy D to C stroller. They seem quite pleased to work with the sound they were given.

Like Leviathan's "Remember The Times", also released in 1969 — another rough-hewn, beat-solid number — "Happy Life" was a little too late to make it. But at least Leviathan had some heaviosity going spare in the lead guitar department.

The Limit reached their zenith with a whisper, rather than a bang.

12. The You-Know-Who Group!!, "(Roses Are Red) My Love" (Casual/4 Corners, 1964)

The title says it all and the song holds no secrets to the connoisseur of beat. I guess this one was included to try to bring home to Blighty and by doing so reclaim some of the effortless recording technique of Merseybeaters, The Undertakers, who had something to do with this tune and the album it came from.

This choppy, minor-key singalong with its pivotal Lennon/McCartney "oohs" is best appreciated for the 34th time while taking in the misty, snowy wonder of the Ouse Valley from Balcombe viaduct.

I'll go to the ends of the earth to hunt down tracks I'm obsessed with, although not literally. But this is not one of them. I've nothing to tell you about this one, apart from it's not all that. I don't trouble myself to collect records any more. I bet the other side's not great, either.

13. Unknown, "Red And Green Talking Machine" (Unreleased, 1967)

On the simplest narrative level, this is simply a melancholic song about a parrot that sits in the corner, chiming up every now and then like a confused old gentleman, "with a beat of his wings".

On the lyric level, the avian red and green talking machine performs a negative function, in this song, to Philip Pullman's daemons in the His Dark Materials trilogy. By reducing a vividly coloured, inquisitive living creature to an automaton, we are invited to regard the singer's own life in similar terms. Without anima — a social life outdoors in collective context — both the man and the bird are captive indoor dwellers, repeating phrases lent them. The singer, perhaps reflecting on his own moral and ethical position, and aware the bird's "not very keen", comments wrily that, "Friends and neighbours say it's cruel, trying to lend him a word or two." But the bird's isolation reflects his loneliness and by teaching the bird a few words when he's on his own with nothing to do, he reaffirms his own existence, in spite of his relative absence in social terms.

Or is the man imprisoned alone, imagining his feathered pal? Or maybe it's a fellow who's so detached he's gone bird, like in "Birdy".

You heard.

14. The Purple Barrier, "Shapes and Sounds" (Eyemark 1011, 1968)

"Shapes and Sounds" is, in the first verse at least, a history song of London. In a way that the faux-zeitgeist maundering of "The Good, The Bad and The Queen" and all psychogeography is not. The Barrier's tune is a revisionary historicist one evoking the lives of people in the city, observed from within at one remove. Albran's pet, in contrast, is a glimpse from outside experience. Whereas The Barrier process the multiple Atlantic cultural crossings through their own class experience and make them understandable in the contemporaneous language of music and culture, Albran's media project is a homage to absence — like Iain Sinclair's London a Rushmore revisioning of erasure in his own image. "The Good, The Bad and The Queen" is a lamentable lament for lost visions of the City, an architectural model of sound carved in a turkey roast. Albran fails to make it.

"Shapes and Sounds" has a folk feel, like the opening tune in The Wicker Man, not just because of the distance between then and now. That's more an effect of the songwriter's awareness of their position in culture. If the Psych Sound is the rediscoverable folk music — the contextual sound, or even the local historical consciousness — of youth in London and the Home Counties at the time, "Shapes and Sounds" is its "Derby Ram". It provides a veritable taxonomy of psycho-tropes, starting with the opening line: "Oh, atoms and colours", progressing to a localist taxonomy or everyday life: "bells, church spires / Each one has a story to tell" - linking the story of the locale with the story of their cosntituent atoms and reflective colours.

The everyday dramas in the song, much influenced by kitchen sinks and flies on walls, speak of the sweetness and gentleness of human relationships as seen on special occasions and in quotidian glances: "O, weddings and love; joy all round / Flowers rising out of the ground". The Barrier's song of acid-illuminated understanding of the linkage between all living things is mediated by a comprehension of the anthropogenic culture in which they are working, which has had a big hand in creating the city ecology they're narrating. The flowers rising from the ground, albeit possibly a weak metaphor for youth activism, stand more effectively for negative cultivation propagated by urban planning, both in respect of unplanned growth of unofficial communities and the natural slippage of floral growth that rises unbidden, even from the most concrete of human endeavours.

The only thing preventing The Purple Barrier from outrunning the planned development of state capitalism in the late-1960s is given away by the line, "Imagine running wild in your head". This is free-thinking at one remove. It recalls the removal of the self from possible confrontation, through fear, apparent in G G Allin's "Outlaw Scumfuk", where he sings about possibly pushing someone off their chair if they persist in upsetting him. But singing about imagining the satisfaction of their desires, The Barrier engage with the imaginary city of past/future, science, literature and politics, simultaneously creating it with others.

15. Anthony Dare's Progress, "Devil" (Unreleased, 1966)

"The sea was black and the sky was green, the devil's hand was red / It was pointing at me since the day I was born, and this is what he said: / 'You're gonna be evil, you're gonna be bad, you're gonna be the devil's son / You're gona hurt everybody your meet and you ain't never gonna have fun.'"

Straight in, first verse, no pissing about, this song's written and performed so heartfelt, it has the patina of an ancient Blues number on it. This is a tough, rough and raw tune, based around a simple, lazy-handed punk riff that's heavy on the storytime stroll-on lariness. But this is no British Blues studio rehash. As might be expected of a song that uses Blues images and paradigms, but enhances them in the retelling, "Devil" commences, rather than starts, with rainswept soundscape with howlin' wind and thunder cracking. These sound effects put "Devil" in either the pop or the early prog camp. I'm plumping for pop. But it's up to you to decide, listeners.

Instrumentation: vox, electric bass, electric organ, drums, gtr., ld. gtr. (fuzz) in chorus.

16. The Information, "Face To The Sun" (Evolution, 1970)

A waltz-time number; sensitive, but not one of those harpsichord ones where you're meant to be whisked into the past for a date with lady fair. This one does the business with some shit-hot drumming and lead picking.

The only other tough beat song in waltz time I'd care to take the time to remember is Michael Leslie's "Make Up Or Break Up", which is so out of kilter and odd-tempo'd you can feel the songwriter mentally keeling over from the re-imagined, re-awakened strain of hard-lived experience.

"Face To The Sun" is about loss, or love coming to be; about getting out of bed and introducing yourself to the morning: "I rise with my face to the sun / Well, I know what has to be done / And I in my heart that we won't be apart / I must go."

Apart from a little bit too much Clapton-influenced Strat-bothering in the mid-riff bit where the singer would be strutting and punching the air, this is a lovely pop tune.

17. Blues & Roots, "Blue Root" (Unreleased, 1964)

Kinda "Shimmy Shimmy Ko-Ko Bop" for a provincial English crowd who'd prefer "Green Onions" any day of the week, this is a pleasingly generic rinky-dink beat instro. It would fulfil most people's expectations of a 60s instrumental, even if they'd never heard one before. In short, it's the generic prototype of the sort of tune played at the start of a set by 60s-influenced bands when starting out. Perfect generic psych! This is an invented tradition caught at the moment of creation. Dontcha know, honky-tonks?

Side B

1. Pink Floyd, "Candy and Currant Bun" (Columbia, 1967)

This is a song about sound. Barrett is having stoned fun with the way his voice sounds with echo on it — like Ol' Dirty Bastard did, and just like the Celestial Empire's singer on "Dragonfly", popping the reverb'd mic — and the rest of the band chip in for emphasis. Barrett and the lads are playing with the sounds, with the words as vocalised orchestral figures. But although the Floyd adhere to the group ethic by adopting a proper name for their collective activity, the separation of the individuals could not be clearer.

And this is not a jazz explosiion. Every instrument plays its part separately, as is clear in the organ break in the middle, the fractured lead gtr lines playing counter melodies and Barrett's wordy dyspraxia. The only shred of the group ethic is the bass/drums nexus, which takes the song from A to B. Even the structure of the song goes against the grain by ignoring the V/C/V/C model and instead keeps things interesting by introducing tension by stringing together a couple of m8s or bridges with intros and stop/start figures.

Barrett's hesitant, mock-cautious sibyllant delivery found a terrible echo in his latter work on Madcap and Barrett. The crazy tension of the song structure is undermined by some cod-surrealist wordplay. But the overall effect of the song is to heighten tension unbearably. Even the slightly naughty, "Please, just f-walk with me" is cringeingly coy, rather than musical-hall saucy, Nothing here of the Bonzos or even the Small Faces. As frightening as "Scream Thy Last Scream", possibly even more so. The reason? The caution and hesitancy about the song's unuttered subtext: living without fear.

2. Unknown, "It's Been A Long Time Coming" (Unknown)

Memorable chorus: "It's been a long time coming, but you've got to hold on / It's been a long time coming, but the past has gone".

Sounds Texan, but after a whole 7.6 minutes looking on the internet, I'm none the wiser about where it was made. If you were to start looking, it'd be a matter of going down the hard road: Rock. US. 1960s.

It's basically a riff on The Just Brothers' "Fried Green Tomatoes", or similar, but the band don't drop the 5th, preferring instead to loon and freak on this classic rhythm and blues-style riff first popularised by John Lee Hooker as "Boogie Chillun", with a harmonica-heavy accompaniment also featuring a guitar with fuzz-tone effect, an electric bass and a drum mix foregrounding a heavy crash cymbal sound.

The song is much concerned with the way poets live, presumably in the hope that something of a poetic cast will rub off. The last line of the last verse says, "we saw things the way the poets said we should". But this is not the end of the matter. There's a direct linkage in the song between words when sung and the transcendental nature of poetry, culminating, in the first couplet in the last verse, in an evocation of industrial collapse and youth activism that has finally succeeded in busting time: "Trains broke and words of truth we sang / The day broke and into the streets we ran".

In this song, rock 'n' roll as a pastime literally becomes a matter of killing time, killing the realism that allows leisure to create only after paid work in someone else's time is done with. The poetic process of abolishing time begins in the second couplet of the first verse: "The words sprang at the start of dawn's decay / The truth sang its song at the break of day". Abandoning the fear of making a living and, well, living, the fellows mark their changed consciousness thus: "Head reeled at screaming waves of doubt / The words move, but mostly shut me out...The white light of the world was at my side". We're with you brother, whenever we hear you sing your song. And you're by our side.

And that's about it for this one. Have a listen and see what you think.

3. Fire, "Flies Like a Bird" (Pye, 1970)

What links "My Father's Name is Dad" by The Fire with The Strawbs's 1970s smash hit "Part of the Union"? One of the latter was in the former, and he's playing on this number from the band's concept LP, "Magic Shoemaker". Here you'll find the story of his shoes and what they do.

Despite the magical nature of the Fire's subject — this is a fantasia on the relative impossibility of creating space for yourself in a creative economy that puts a high price on space — there's a nagging, nay-saying voice in the song that constantly asserts its refusal to believe the evidence of its own eyes: that a man can "know who he wants to know" and, what is more, fly like a bird in the sky. What's the point of a magical narrative if you can't supersede retarded realities in it? With this nay-saying parental voice in the foreground, the Fire effectively smother their story of social mobility before it has a chance to get going.

There's a sense in which the song mourns the loss of freedom of movement and freedom of association available only in the fairy past to Levellers, chapbook sellers, itinerants, charcoal burners, etc. The lads involved in this concept LP would have been better advised to do something about their present condition, rather than harp on about flying in dreamland. I guess they atoned somewhat with the aforementioned Strawbs single.

On a musical-contextual note, the song features a gtr. figure reminiscent of the one that cuts through Skip Bifferty's "On Love". On a literary note, "He Flies Like a Bird" is really about the song-process and story-telling, rather than the story of the shoes as an allegory for social mobility. It's a jolly enough number, but if you want a yarn about joy in the face of impossibility, you'd be better off having a listen to "Cutting a Rug" by the man from Australia who calls himself Youngie Doug. But not necessarily happier after the last chord dies away.

4. Sharon Tandy & Fleur De Lys, "Hold On" (Atlantic, 1967)

Better by far than the too-heavy Ipssissimus version, which is ponderous and no fun. Sharon whispers and half-talks her way through this discotheque-busting number in 'sexy' mode, but it's a real perfomance. Fortunately, her laid-back hushing tempers the over-amped, string-pinging, fret-bothering youths responsible for the later heavy version — for it is they — into giving their tune a nice soulful spin. It's got some funk to it, this one, courtesy of the electric guitarist, who seems to have lost his way on the journey to Ipssissimus.

5. The Buzz, "You're holding me down" (Columbia, 1966)

Produced by The Guv'nor. No, not Lenny McLean the East London knuckle man unbeaten on the cobbles. We're talking Joe Meek, the cat-loving, ex-RAF technician and sound genius. This is yer actual ex-girlfriend put-down number, Scotch-style, from the pens and pick-ups of the Boston Dexters, blue-eyed Keltic fringe-flippers, soulsters and oat-rocking daddys.

These fellers were Primal Screaming from around the year Gillespie was first born. This song's got the best guitar stabs ever. This is surely the tune that compelled Phil Smee to invent the retroactive term "Freakbeat" to describe beat tunes with a hip twist. There's a dynamic, exciting footstomp intro and, even more compelling, an extended freak-outro, picking out and looping the words "GO BACK!" from the chorus throat-wrenchingly bellowed and then amplified to the front of the recording, over a howling backing featuring over-trebled amp, reproducing an onstage extended jam that the DJs could cut so as not to upset or overexcite their listeners.

As it goes, the DJs and their shadowy cultural masters decided to cut the whole song from the playlists, which is the reason most people worldwide haven't heard this wonderful waxing, channelling all the emotion out of Scotland in the the 1960s in one performance. The last words are, "Get out of my life! I don't love you no more!" And that's that.

6. The Fairytale, "Listen To Mary Cry" (Decca, 1967)

A funny, sparse arrangement for this one that matches the evocation of loneliness in the words. A remarkably restrained, professional-style, performance for your average vox/back. vox/organ/bass/gtr/drums combo, It's so restrained. But it's also powerful because of this restraint.

Once again, in the form of the arrangement and the way the melody intertwines with the beat, we encounter the eldritch influence of our old friends, The Seeds. This time, it's out front in a major way, with an A to G riff dancing merrily with itself with a bit of raga to keep it company. Meanwhile, in the background, the other chaps in the group emphasise and accent the words "love her" on occasions, to lighten the tone. If you doubt that emphasis and accent are two separate things, listen to this tune before correcting me. Also again, the words are trying to evoke a poetic milieu beyond beat music.

I wonder if any of the generic psych songwriters I'm commenting on published poetry at the time, or later on. Anyway, that's as maybe — we're trying to get to grips with this tune at the moment, thanks very much. The effortlessness of this tune is its attraction. You can dance to it — I've managed it successfully — nod your head to it, look out of a train window thinking about something else while enjoying its mellifluousness. All sorts. A good all-rounder, this one. At the risk of going all 'pop', I'll give it foive.

7. The Poets, "Wooden Spoon" (Decca, 1967)

Seeing them in their frock coats, Prince Valiant haircuts and what-not, you'd be forgiven for mistaking them at first glance for no-talent, peruked boff-meisters, The Snobs, But no: The Poets are great players and arrangers and they made good records out of Scotland.

The Poets have been championed for their great songs in the past few years by Lenny Helsing from the Lairds of Leith, otherwise known as The Thanes, and formerly of The Green Telescope. Helsing put together a compilation of The Poets' loveliest numbers a couple of years ago.

"Wooden Spoon" is a souly poetic blast about running hard to keep up in a 7-day working week, coming last and dealing with it, recognising that you can't win by struggling to keep up. As if that weren't enough, the singer's singing that other people "live in stately houses, while I've fought to stay alive".

We're in the territory of the literary outsider, populated by gangs of sensitive alientated youths at the time The Poets were doin' it. Thursday's Children, Willy the Wild One. But The Poets are more white collar — or, more accurately, white frilly collar — than the many blue collar angry men elsewhere in the music biz. Nevertheless, despite their more refined commentary, they don't resort to setting themselves above the rest of us by virtue of their aspirational poetical prowess. All the time, we're being urged not to forget that, notwithstanding the need to keep focused on acting positively, there are some things outside our control: "This cloud of degradation always hangs above my mind". And that is? The aspirational swamp. Let's avoid it then, and get on to the playing of the song.

The verse riff is quite like Gene Vincent's "Bird-doggin'" and there are echoes of The Kinks in the chord progressions. But this is no straight-ahead stage-to-studio beat number. There's a degree of "oo-oo-ee-oo-oo" that owes something to The Action's way of constructing immediately pretty counter melodies, but the rest of the tune showcases all their own style. And the drum sound takes it into the era of Heavy or Prog. There's a great bit where the singer goes, "I gotta run!", then the band drops out for a couple of beats and he does a two-beat puff-and-pant combo. Very nice. My favourite bit, apart from the whole rest of the song, is when twin dive-bomber lead gtrs — double golden eagle guitars, no less — swoop in to strafe the middle 8.

8. The Fairytale, "Guess I Was Dreaming" (Decca, 1967)

This one fades in, with lone drums. Then the rest of the orchestration moves in: vox/deep organ/thin gtr/piano accents.

This has to be the song that inspired Withnail & I. Either that, or Bruce Robinson made the whole thing up himself. You the audience decide. Come to think of it, if anything it's more like a colourful version of "Waiting for the Man": "Here he comes, walking thru my mind / With so many colours, making me blind. / One-eyed midget by his side / He started fusing my eyes." Yes, it's about the old dirty rugs. The character in the song, either with or without his co-dependents, has been "Watching, waiting, looking over my front wall". Each chorus ends with a refrain of "Guess I was dreaming, guess I was dreaming... so bad".

To cut a short story long, it's a dealer song, just like the Velvet Underground's more famous one or my favourite of the genre, The Seeds's "Mr Tripmaker".

[Technical note: Slight bit of drop-out in the 2nd from last chorus.]

9. Les Sauterelles, "Dream Machine" (Blick, 1968)

Les sauterelles sont des insectes orthoptères communs presque partout dans le monde et qui se déplacent en sautant à l'aide de leurs longues pattes postérieures.

This song, which is to my knowledge the best Swiss pop-psych tune ever recorded, narrates a vivid memory of someone else's childhood, probably located in the past, which is where a lot of this sort of thing tends to happen in songs. There's shades of Proust here, in the protagonist's precise self-positioning, or obsession leaning towards nostalgia, his insistence on the crystal clear constancy of memory: "I'll remember all the time". Not that I've read anything by Proust — or Henry James, for that or any other matter.

The nearest psych analogs are Pinkerton's Assorted Colors' "Magic Rocking Horse". Or John Holt's "Ali Baba". More the former than the latter, though, if you're after grid references. There's a twang in the singer's accent that made me think he was Dutch, before I used the internet to find out more. But in my ignorance he could just have easily been French, Italian, German or Swedish.

On the music side, the beat's carried along by a heavy tambourine and a fuzz lead does the counter-melody nicely. Towards the end, the whole song is brought to a halt for a couple of bars, with a music box chiming "La Vie En Rose", as warbled originally by Edith Piaf, winding down through a slow fade, before they bring the song back and finish it with another melody altogether.

10. The Attack, "Lady Orange Peel" (Decca, 1968)

Quite some musical ensemble this lot got together. Rhythm gtr./drums (up in the mix)/vox/back. vox/piano/bass/lead gtr. A strict groove is imposed on proceedings, set by the metronome-like drums. It's the sort of thing stupid people sample to make their half-baked ideas seem more dynamic when in fact they've just added some beat to a melody that came along while they were waiting to make their next shit.

I don't like this tune. Not for the reason I've just mentioned, though. That would be plain crazy. I just don't like it. It's not so much the strictness that bothers me — I like the way that the freakout fuzz lead gtr. is constrained by reverb and the need to always return to the stone groove — as the attempted masculinisation of generic psych, which is essentially a louche genre, not a butch one.

Let me illustrate. The line, "Come into my garden and I'll peel a pear for you" is not at all inviting — if indeed this is, as I suspect, intended as a come-on song. In fact, it's a form of verbal strutting, which is most unappealing. It's the sort of thing Plant would have nicked off of someone good and done worse.

I rest my case.

[Technical note: Slight drop-out just two lines from the end.]

11. The Poets, "In Your Tower" (Decca, 1967)

Christian must have had a thing about The Poets at the time he did this tape for me.

Despite the first words being, "Wench, you'd better watch your master", I get the impression that this is ironic. Taken as a whole, which is how artefacts should be taken, the song is a genuine warning against the dangers of lovestruck folly. It's about what'll happen if you let yourself be put on a pedestal: the strange, unfortunate man worshipping you will come to take this as a sign of moral weakness and will lock the unfortunate lady up in her very own tower. That's what the fairytale Rapunzel is all about.

I guess the split with the ex left The Poets's songwriter with a deeper appreciation of the ways of love. It's certainly a more human approach than the one popularised by The Rolling Stones on many occasions. I'd like to hear more stuff written by this person. He's got something of the all-sides-of-argument songwriter about him, like Mickey Newbury. Instrumentation: gtr./bass/drums/vox/flute (or occarina).

[Technical note: A touch of accidental "Rec" button over the 2nd bar.]

12. Kaleidoscope, "Dive Into Yesterday" (Mercury, 1967)

A paragon of ambiguity, this tune, until someone tells me about some Ugly Things interview, or similar, that I've not seen, in which the band reveals that it was about something less good. Given the opening line, "Since his disappearance through the smoke rings of our time", this one could be about Michael Moorcock's zeitgeist anti-hero, Jerry Cornelius or even Syd Barrett. I detect something of a Barrett tribute in the vocal style. That's to be expected, though, at the time. Just think of all the late-70s characters, including proper punk rockers with their own great songs and styles, not to mention all the assorted tossers, who took to rolling their "r"s like Lydon. Even Poly Styrene did it, and she was the neutron bomb.

In any event, there are heavy hints of Pink Floyd in the off-kilter crescendo and diminuendo and the melodic and counter-melodic progressions and regressions. Stop me, I can't go on. And the time-change in the chorus. The Kaleidoscope is a much better name under which to do this sort of thing, though.

Anyway, onwards! Listening to "Dive Into Yesterday" with my eyes shut tight as the train goes through the avenue of railway trees approaching Haywards Heath from the south, the colours playing under my eyelids, nature's own dream machine reminds me why I like psych.

Unsurprisingly, the glowering shade of Dylan pops up, especially in the use of the Dylanine extended line, viz. "Microscopic tambourines are tickling your ears" and "Relax your eyes, for after all, we can but share these minutes". He's also there in various extended surrealistical similes: "Battalions in baby blue are bursting red balloons / The water pistols are all filled with lemonade." The last line of that blank couplet picks out a thread left hanging in the air after ludic political affrays in The USA, France and elsewhere.

If you've got a water pistol, fill it with lemonade.

13. Unknown, "Can't Stop The Want I Got For You Babe" (Unknown)

Sandy Sarjeant did the original of this tune, which first made its way on to a compilation courtesy of the "Beat Club '67" LP (Polydor, 1967). It was co-written by Graham Bonney out of RGM no-hits The Riot Squad, under his real surname. Judging from the black and white clip of her performing this number on Beat Club, which is on and off YouTube like a celebrity relationship, Sarjeant was one of the most energetic dancers ever to grace the stage. Her bendy-leg dancing and rubbish miming to this number is one of those images that'll stay with you forever. Sandy married Ian McLagan, the Small Faces' kbd., but, strangely, this single never came out on Immediate. Probably not fey enough or something.

Unknown's version is a cheek-blistering fuzz-feast straight outta Shoutsville. With a hairy cock on it. More on-the-knees pleading than The Troggs at their most beggingist. More bridled lust than Kenneth Connor. Much better than White Ape's heavy twin-gtr. 2004 stab at it.

14. The Exiles, "Love In The Making" (Oak, 1965)

A simple teenage try-out, this one, reminiscent of the simple progressions and ABC bass/treble interplay of The Game's "I Turn to Love You" (Oak Records, 1967) that echo the imaginary Brit-teen concerns of yestersong.

This one's about a two-way teenage lust that's just searching for a place and time to be fulfilled. It could work for a male or female voice. This time, it's a lad singing.

15. The Birds, "How Can it Be?" (Decca, 1965)

It was only after Ron Wood, brother of the more musical Art of Artwood Combo jazz fame, a 'hot' music group that still wows newly invented/created Mods all over the place after they've got bored with the strident and fed-up with the obvious, joined Ian Stewart's backing band, that they got a modicum of the funk that they ever possessed. Having listened to "How Can It Be?" 253 times, I can say with some assurance that it's more of everything than the Stones' ever managed. It makes The Creation's entire oeuvre sound like the (pre-1980) Human League in comparison.

Also, the sloppy bass line is the figure isolated and niched by The Eyes for the monumental "You're Too Much". Or was it the other way round?

This is the answer song — I wish people still did them — to The Contours's "First I Look At The Purse". In The Birds's number, the voice is a wondering what he did wrong to deserve such bad treatment.

In the driving seat, there's a bouncy, Ike Turnerene lead/rhythm gtr line played with as little left hand movement as possible. It's played the way the Blues is played. It could've been lifted from a Funkadelic track. In fact, it's more likely that the F-boys nicked it from Ron and the Birds. And probably the idea that men could have ladies' haircuts, too. And it wouldn't be going too far to say you could take the drummer to the Bank 'o' Funk and swap him for a wheelbarrow fulla gold.

Layzngem, I gotta a hardon for this track. Well, as near a stiffy as I can get these days, what with fear of nukeular devices in luggage, poison terrorists, street stabbings, ageing, and the drip drip of sherry damage to my loins over the years. Phew! Help me up one time!! I wanna boogie again!!!

A great harp solo divides the first and second movements, then, so quick and neat you couldn't push a breath between them, Ron commences to pick out such a lazy, hungover gtr solo it's hard to see where he got it from in a milieu that was getting down to perfection in pop. And it ends with a reverb chord: SNAP! {RVB!} SNAP!

16. Ipsissimus, "Hold On" (Parlophone, 1969)

The only difference between this version and Sharon Tandy's club-happy, stomping side is that this is a lot worse. Each verse starts with lugubrious Fuzz-Wah, or Wazz, announcing the tune's, not to mention the band's, utter heaviness. And it's durability. They want us to know they can play it pop or rock.

In fact, Metal vocalists searching for the roots of The Screech, or anything to do with their yen for heaviosity, could do worse than check this track. Ted Zeppelin came later.

A couple of times, the pick-up clicking extremity of the fuzz-tone on the lead gtr soloing has got on my nerves to the extent that I've considered locking and loading a different tape in my SONY TCM-200DV "casssette-corder". But the end of the solo is so well signposted that it's over before too long. And, fortunately, the tape runs out before this song, so everyones's almost happy: the boys get to finish their performance of their tune the way they always wanted to do it — and they're still playing somewhere in the past, from the point this tape runs out — and I get to turn the cassette over and continue with the musical mind expansion hip trip on the flip.

It Is Not Written

- Chesterfield Kings: Preening Prannies or Keepers of the Secret Flame?
- Taking Weak Tea in the Elysian Fields of Whimsy. A reprise of my musings on C86, the backgarden of rock and roll; the final part of this epic tribute to the most useless prissy foppish rock bores ever
- Secret Gigs: A Badly Hidden History of Covert Rock 'n' Roll
- Bang! Magazine (recollections of the famous Ipswich counterculture pre-zine zine)
- Bent Magician. The True Story
- Made-Up Bands: Who's Foolin' Who?
- Rock 'n' roll as Anthropogenesis: Creating Ecologies Beyond Identity

Gitusmthin else
Your Editor

Rockhaunter

No. 3, Undated

Doo-Wop Shambhala

Originally a B-side to "The Lonely One", Sheriff and The Ravel's "Shombalor" (1959, Vee-Jay Records, 306) is a massive slab of on-the-spot mic poetry, otherwise known as Doo-Wop. A different spelling of "Shombolar" was used on Songs The Cramps Taught Us, Volume One (2001). It's possible that the song name printed on the original Vee-Jay record label was a mis-spelling of what the group called their tune: it certainly sounds like "hombolar" when they sing it. I'm sticking with The Cramps' revisionist version of "Shombolar"

I'm guessing that Sheriff and The Ravels were a black group, because that's the Doo Wop demography if not its constituency, and I'd say they were from Chicago, because Vee-Jay was based there. But I don't know for sure. They've a heavy, steady rockabilly sound — probably why The Cramps dug the disc — anchored on slap bass, rim-shot drums, treble guitar and, I think, a tinkle of piano in the background. Beyond the bass undertones, the vocals including the lead are mid-range and don't venture into the outer space tones of, say, The Four Seasons' Frankie Valli. The guitar intro, flamenco-ing octaves up and down in double-quick time, is worth the price of admission.

I first heard "Shombolar" on Songs The Cramps Taught Us, Volume One and it immediately jumped ahead of The Chips' "Rubber Biscuit" (1956, Josie Records, Josie 803) in my mind's ear. "Shombolar", like "Rubber Biscuit", has running through it echoes of reform school marching rhymes (see books in a library for more on The Chips). Its "Go left, right, left, right" refrain and the lines, "I love left foot stomp and-a right foot drag, 'n-a / Hey it's good to march!" add a layer of reflexive sharpness to the song's expression of culture and make the cultural link between Doo Wop and the criminal justice system even more explicit than The Chips' rhythmic-linguistic allusions do. "Shombolar" is as much a prison song as Sam Cooke's later and more famous tune, "Chain Gang" (1960, RCA Victor, 47-7783).

Either way of spelling/ pronouncing "Shombalor" is similar enough to Shambhala, the mythopoeical predecessor to the fictional Shangri-la, to merit mention. Maybe there was a girl with an ebonic phonetic moniker involved. This usage may even be a popular memory trace of the 1930s and 40s fictional comic book and radio crime fighter, The Shadow, who was trained in mystical Shamballah. Even though The Shadow radio programme went off air in 1954, there is evidence that his influence persisted in rockin n rollin minds. Link Wray used The Shadow's sinister moralising catchphrase, "Who knows what evil lurks in the hearts of men? The Shadow knows!" at the start of his instrumental "The Shadow Knows" (1964, Swan Records, S-4171). Or perhaps members of the vocal group came across Shambhala in contemporaneous references to the Dalai Lama's escape from Tibet and into India on 31 March 1959, which was all over the news, and incorporated it as a motif in their new tune.

Check the archive of the internet entity know as The Hound for "Shombolar": hear this howlin' rave and die! Alternatively, Songs the Cramps Taught Us, Volume One is still available from all good record shops. You can even get "Shombalor" legitimately for the first time outside of the vintage record racks, since it was reissued on the Vee-Jay Definitive Collection LP in August 2007. I imagine that the sleeve notes on the latter would provide a much needed supplement to this speculative post.

In an attempt to enhance your listening experience, I've transcribed the words as I hear them. I'd be happy to accept plausible suggestions for alterations.

Shombolar Lyrics
Interpretation Version,
Nowhere Near Definitive

Go left, right, left right
Go left, right, left right
Go left, right, left right
Go left, right, left right
(Oh lady) Shombolar (Oh lady) Shombolar
(Oh lady) chickenin' out and then a-root for it, chicken 'n-a, Shombolar
Baby, d'y'wanna move out, do it now? Ya gettin' on the countdown, please?
Baby, wha' the fuck do you need, now? Ya gettin' on the catfish knees?
'n-ah, I love swing-ding, Rickey-bing you're a healthy one, hubba!
And it's known to some that-a jigga-wah I love pick-'em-up and lay-'em-down
(Oh lady) Shombolar, (Oh lady) Shombolar
(Oh lady) chickenin' out and then a-root for it, chicken 'n-a, Shombolar
And it's gonna: Wine-o Buy-No frees Jackie Frankenstein-oh
Maybe Jackie came to dine, 'n-a forgettin' on he stole my wine,
'n-a, asks George "You bing, you bong, you bong?"
Leaves Jimmy Jones, he skipped to one, a-hubba
And it's known to some that-a jigga-wah I love pick-'em-up and lay-'em-down
(Oh lady) Shombolar, (Oh lady) Shombolar
(Oh lady) chickenin' out and then a-root for it, chicken 'n-a, Shombolar

Chorus

Of all the animals in the world, I'd rather be a bear (Raar!)
Climb the highest mountain, double to the rear
(Oh lady) Shombolar, (Oh lady) Shombolar
(Oh lady) chickenin' out and then a-root for it, chicken in-a, Shombolar
I love fat man mambo, baby, do the king of the jungle,
You can only get it from the Congo. And you try to get it definitely
I love left foot stomp and-a right foot drag, 'n-a, hey it's good to march!
And it's known to some that-a jigga-wah I love pick-'em-up and lay-'em-down
(Oh lady) Shombolar, (Oh lady) Shombolar
(Oh lady) chickenin' out and then a-root for it, chicken 'n-a, Shombolar

Chorus

Of all the animals in the world, I'd rather be a bear (Raar!)
Climb the highest mountain, double to the rear.
(Oh lady) Shombolar, (Oh lady) Shombolar
(Oh lady) Chickenin' out and then a-root for it, chicken 'n-a, Shombolar
Go left, right, left right
[to fade, in a call-response duet with the lead singer]

INDEX

please note

n indicates relevant page number(s)

ROCKHAUNTER

CONCEPTUAL GAIETY IN SOUND & VISION

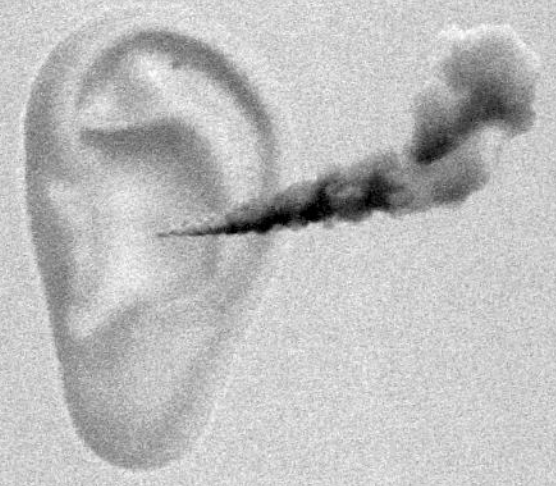

HAUNTIQUARIANISM NOT HAUNTOLOGY

DEAD VILLAGES: HORROR, SUFFERING & LOCALITY

THE WEIRD & THE UNEXPLAINED, PART 1

75p

Lightning Source UK Ltd.
Milton Keynes UK
UKHW050750110419
340868UK00005B/747/P

9 780987 412225